PRACTICING
RECONCILIATION
in a
VIOLENT WORLD

PRACTICING RECONCILIATION in a VIOLENT WORLD

Michael Battle

morehouse

HARRISBURG • LONDON

Unless otherwise noted, all scriptural quotations in this book are from the New Revised Standard Version Bible. Copyright © 1989 by the Division of Christian Education of the National Council of the Churches of Christ in the United States of America. Used by permission. All rights reserved.

Morehouse Publishing, P.O. Box 1321, Harrisburg, PA 17105

Morehouse Publishing, The Tower Building, 11 York Road, London SE1 7NX

Morehouse Publishing is a Continuum imprint.

Cover art copyright © Superstock, Inc./Superstock

Cover design by Wesley Hoke

Library of Congress Cataloging-in-Publication Data

Battle, Michael, 1963–
    Practicing reconciliation in a violent world / Michael Battle.
        p. cm.
    Includes bibliographical references.
    ISBN 0-8192-2109-0 (pbk.)
    1. Reconciliation—Religious aspects—Christianity. 2. Violence—Religious aspects—Christianity. I. Title.
    BT736.4.B38 2005
    261.8'32—dc22
                                    2004021951

Printed in the United States of America

05 06 07 08 09   10 9 8 7 6 5 4 3 2 1

CONTENTS

CHAPTER 1
Reconciling a Violent World

"Some people will say it's velocity or physics that put it there. To me, it's an act of God," said Silecchia, who cried for twenty minutes after his discovery.

Silecchia, a Christian, found several crosses standing upright in the smoldering wreckage of the September 11 attack on the World Trade Center towers. The "crosses" were crossbeams that had fallen from the top of the collapsing north tower that had landed in an unusual position. Believing them to be a sign from God, Silecchia dubbed the area "God's House," and he called distraught rescue workers there to pray. Word spread as clergy ministering on the site encountered the structures and told others about them.

Silecchia led a priest, Father Brian Jordan, to the site. "It was astounding," Jordan said. "When he showed it to me, I was an instant believer."

Silecchia told the priest that the crosses should be saved for a permanent memorial. Jordan agreed, and contacted Deputy Mayor Joseph Lhota to make arrangements. The most significant of the crosses was removed from the wreckage, affixed by ironworkers to a permanent base, and then placed on the high walkway over West Street. Some three hundred people gathered there for prayer and reflection. Firefighters came. Police officers came. Construction workers, rescue personnel, Port Authority officers, and others—all gathered at the foot of the twenty-feet-tall cross to watch Father Jordan, a Franciscan friar, bless the cross and pray for "the healing mercy of God on all Americans."

"Behold the glory of the cross at ground zero," Jordan said. "This is our symbol of hope, our symbol of faith, our symbol of healing."

The workers prayed and sang "God Bless America" together before returning to work. A teary-eyed firefighter said that the cross helped him overcome his anger. "We thought the devil was here, but with this cross, we know God is here," the firefighter said.[1]

Knowing that God is present, even in the midst of something that looks more like the devil's work—that's reconciliation. And it is the work that you and I are called to do in this world. "But I say to you that listen, Love your enemies, do good to those who hate you, bless those who curse you, pray for those who abuse you. If anyone strikes you on the cheek, offer the other also . . ." (Luke 6:27–29). That's what Jesus says. Nice words, but what do we actually do with them? Did Jesus really mean that we should literally turn the other cheek and let someone hit us again?

How do we practice reconciliation in a violent world? This question haunts me, and perhaps it haunts you as well. How does one love a coworker who seems hell-bent on sabotaging a successful career? How does one make peace with a spouse in the midst of a broken marriage? And how do religious people resolve differences when religious interpretations seem to lead to righteous indignation rather than to reconciliation?

Jesus' words seem impossibly difficult to enact. We become like a little boy, frightened in the night. He screams, so his mother comes into his room to comfort him. "It's okay," she says to her son, "God is with you, even in the dark." The little boy's response echoes one any of us might make: "But Mommy, I want someone with skin on."

"Put some skin on those words, Jesus," we too want to say. "Show me what reconciliation looks like. Be practical, Jesus, because I'd be killed if I listened to you."

I went looking for God with skin on in 1988. I was in seminary at Princeton, and I was given a grant to spend the summer in India. I spent half the summer in Bombay (now known as Mumbai) observing a Christian social work agency in Dharavi, still the largest slum area in the world according to Western sociologists. The other half of the summer I went on pilgrimage to see God with skin on. For me that meant going to see Mother Teresa and the work she did. Feeding the *harajan* or children of God, washing the mucus and feces off the sick, and playing with colicky infants— these were some of the ways she ministered to Christ's body. I arrived in Calcutta by train, late in the day, exhausted. My exhaustion deepened as I saw human horses running through the streets carrying people from the upper caste or class.

I woke up the next morning at 5:00 a.m. to go to matins, or morning prayer, and pray with Mother Teresa. Being in the presence of someone who had become like a rock star to me felt like a dream. "What's the most important thing in the spiritual life?" I asked her. She said, "To pray." And she concluded, "Not just with words." It was not quite the concrete answer that I wanted.

Mother Teresa came to the United States in 1990. She was attending a meeting in Boston. Someone stood up at the end of her talk and asked, "Mother, since there is a sharp decline in religious vocations, especially in women's orders, can you tell me the secret of why the Order of the Missionaries of Charity continues to grow?"

Mother Teresa responded, "I give them Jesus."

"But Mother, I wonder if you offer a certain technique, such as requiring the sisters to always wear their habits, or . . . "

Mother Teresa interrupted, "I give them Jesus."

"Yes Mother, we are all aware of your profound work, but I'm asking about something different . . . something else."

Mother Teresa responded, "I give them Jesus; there is nothing else."

I told this story in the Church of the Holy Family in Chapel Hill, North Carolina, where I once served as an assistant priest. I got an e-mail from a parishioner praising me for the profound story, but she asked, "How do I give Jesus?" Her question—the question we all want to ask—returns us to the original question: How does one practice the ideals of Jesus? How, in the world, can we love our enemies and be reconciled?

My only answer to these questions is to say that we must inhabit reconciliation. There is nothing else. In Western culture today we so often focus on inviting God into our lives—as if God weren't there already. The story we tell is the "me and God" story. But if we are going to be reconciling people, we must learn to accept God's invitation to inhabit the Holy One's life. The goal of created life is to inhabit God rather than to focus on God's inhabiting us. "So we are ambassadors for Christ, since God is making his appeal through us; we entreat you on behalf of Christ, be reconciled to God. For our sake God made Christ to be sin who knew no sin, so that in Christ "we might become the righteousness of God" (2 Corinthians 5:20–21), writes St. Paul. We are invited to be in Christ—to become the righteous of God, to inhabit God—by reconciling what has broken us. We're invited to engage in Christian spiritual practices, to use our imaginative abilities to overcome provincial thinking, and to reconcile the brokenhearted. Ultimately, what we are all called to offer each other is God's reconciling love for the world in which we all live and in which we can even flourish.

In this book, I hope to paint a picture of what inhabiting God looks like (especially for Christians in the so-called developed world, who may not be aware of irreconcilable differences on a global scale). The current and global tensions between conservatives and liberals, Muslim and Christian, rich and poor, those of color and those called white, women and men, and homosexual and heterosexual cannot simply be resolved by coming to consensus, for such a consensus will never occur. Our work as Christians is to will reconciliation as Christ did and to recognize that reconciliation is a slow and arduous process. It doesn't happen overnight, but it won't happen at all unless we begin. Willing that reconciliation, engaging in spiritual practices that promote it, thinking creatively about ways to reconcile with others—these and other practices honor Christ and the ways he operates in the world—nonviolently and forever focused on reconciliation. Practicing reconciliation puts skin on God.

Though it doesn't always sound like it, this slow and arduous work is good news because we no longer have to think of reconciliation as a term paper that we have to write ourselves and turn in on time. Think of it as an oak tree growing from a small seedling into a large tree, a process that takes many years and happens only when water, sun, and nutrients are provided. God provides—God wills—the conditions that make growth in reconciliation possible, just as God provides the nutrients the oak seedling needs to grow. That this miracle belongs to God, however, doesn't let us off the hook. The oak tree can grow without human assistance, but God needs our hands and feet and words to bring about reconciliation.

Being a reconciling person—enacting reconciliation on earth— also requires openness to God's work within us. We can participate in the process of reconciliation. We can even commit ourselves to actively engage in practices that help us become more reconciling as people. But ultimately, the final work is God's, and it will be enacted if we cooperate in the process. And God is always larger and more capable than we can expect or imagine.

I discovered that for myself one morning in Cardiff, Wales. It was a Sunday morning and, having grown up in the Bible Belt of the southern United States, I knew that it was time to go to church. The bells were tolling, and I knew they tolled, in part, for me. I departed my bed and breakfast accommodations and hit the cobblestone streets in search of a church, not sure of where I'd find a church. Fortunately, God's messenger arrived—or so I thought. He was a young black guy walking down the cobblestones ahead of me. Another black guy in Wales was enough of an anomaly for me to believe that God had a hand in the "coincidence." He carried a guitar and was out walking at church time, so I deduced that through him God was leading me to church.

I followed him as best I could, hoping that he would lead me to a bustling community church, full of young people, music, and a social gospel. And then a car pulled alongside my angel from God. He got in and they drove away.

I was devastated and felt abandoned. But it was church time and I had to go. Like Pavlov's dog, I was obedient to the tolling bell and wandered into an Anglican church with cold seats that felt like stone. Only a smattering of folks dotted the massive Gothic edifice, mostly elderly women with what looked like purple hair. As I reflect on what was about to become my epiphany, the Borg, the enemy on the television show *Star Trek: The Next Generation*, comes to mind. Those villains, the Borg, were so confident in their military prowess that a stranger could board their ship and they wouldn't even acknowledge his or her presence unless they perceived it as an imminent threat. As I sat in that cold, hard, Gothic church, I felt like Borg surrounded me. No one acknowledged my presence unless I tried to speak to him or her (or sit next to one of them). I, as a young African American male, tried my hardest to avoid presenting myself as a threat to their established, white, British, traditional world. To make matters worse, the preacher that day spoke about the efficacy of used cars—and I think he actually tried to sell his own during the service. There were no references to the day's biblical lessons or to the Gospel in his sermon. I felt like I was in T. S. Eliot's "Wasteland." Even so, God picked this most unlikely place for my epiphany. It was there, with the purple-haired Borg, that I heard my call to the priesthood.

It's hard for me to imagine a more unlikely scenario. One is supposed to hear God calling you through great passion and conviction. Isn't that the way it's supposed to happen? Something dramatic is supposed to occur, something like a burning bush, an angel with an annunciation. And yet, God's call came to me in a church that felt wholly alien instead of nourishing. It was as if that Borg-like Anglican church in Wales was the only setting in which God could speak to me about the needs of the world and not just about my own needs.

God works, as they say, in mysterious ways, as well as in mysterious times and places. Sometimes the Borg—the enemy—is actually the angel of annunciation if we're willing to be open and attentive. Reconciliation is all around us if we are willing to inhabit it because God has already reconciled us. Paul explains, "So if anyone is in

Christ, there is a new creation: everything old has passed away; see, everything has become new! All this is from God, who [has already] reconciled us to himself through Christ, and has given us the ministry of reconciliation" (2 Corinthians 5:17–18). God has already reconciled us through Christ. Our task is to practice the presence of Christ and live (inhabit) such divine life—not as some utopian vision. But as concrete reality.

CHAPTER 2
A *Typology of Reconciliation*

Some centuries ago, the Pope decided that all the Jews had to leave the Vatican. Naturally, there was a big uproar from the Jewish community. So the Pope made a deal. He would have a religious debate with a member of the Jewish community. If the Jew won, the Jews could stay. If the Pope won, the Jews would have to leave.

The Jews realized that they had no choice. So they picked a middle-aged man named Moishe to represent them. Moishe asked for one change to the debate. To make it more interesting, neither side would be allowed to talk. The Pope agreed.

The day of the great debate came. Moishe and the Pope sat opposite each other for a long time before the Pope raised his hand and showed three fingers. After several moments of reflection, Moishe looked back at him and raised one finger.

The Pope thought about Moishe's response and then waved his fingers in a circle around his head. Looking a little angry, Moishe pointed to the ground where he sat. The Pope, appearing a little frustrated, pulled out a wafer and a glass of wine. With little thought, Moishe pulled out an apple.

The Pope stood up and said, "I give up. This man is too good. The Jews can stay."

An hour later, the cardinals were all around the Pope asking him what happened. The Pope said: "First I held up three fingers to represent the Trinity. He responded by holding up one finger to remind me that there was still one God common to both our religions. Then I waved my finger around me to show him that God was all around us. He responded by pointing to the ground and showing that God was also right here with us. I pulled out the wine and the wafer to show that God absolves us from our sins. He pulled out an apple to remind me of original sin. He had an answer for everything. What could I do?"

Meanwhile, the Jewish community had crowded around Moishe. "What happened?" they asked. "Well," said Moishe, "First he said to me that the Jews had three days to get out of here. I told him that not one of us was leaving. Then he told me that this whole city would be cleared of Jews. I let him know that we were staying right here."

"And then?" asked a woman.

"I don't know," said Moishe. "He took out his lunch and I took out mine."

The joke illustrates one of the most ignored truths about reconciliation: each of us sees through a lens constructed from the events and lessons of our own lives. Our own lives. Not the life of the person across the table from us. And that often prevents us from listening to each other and actually hearing what another person believes or feels. Maybe it seems obvious to you, but in my own experience, it's a source of deep misunderstanding and of our unwillingness to reconcile with each other. If you'll humor me for a bit, let me show you how much difference your own lens can make.

Before we wade through my more elaborate typology of reconciliation, I ask you first to take this short survey. This isn't a test with right or wrong answers. The survey is simply a tool to help you recognize the ways in which you personally approach reconciliation. Read each statement below and circle the answer that most closely approximates your response: Y (yes), N (no), or P (possibly).

1. Do you greet and make eye contact with strangers?   Y   N   P
2. Do you curse or swear more naturally than you bless or inspire?   Y   N   P
3. Do you initiate forgiveness?   Y   N   P
4. Do you have enemies who wish you harm?   Y   N   P
5. Do you have relationships such that people would risk their lives for you?   Y   N   P
6. Do you find enjoyment from gossip or another's misery?   Y   N   P
7. Do you think there are unforgivable sins?   Y   N   P
8. Do you believe in capital punishment?   Y   N   P
9. Have you ever been forgiven?   Y   N   P
10. Are you prone to inflicting wrath on others?   Y   N   P
11. Are you prone to inflicting wrath on yourself?   Y   N   P
12. Do you believe hell is forever?
13. Do you believe God will eventually save everyone?   Y   N   P
14. Do you believe a certain ethnic group is more spiritual?   Y   N   P
15. Do you avoid conflict?   Y   N   P
16. Are children better peacemakers than adults?   Y   N   P
17. Are women better peacemakers than men?   Y   N   P
18. Do you have a pet?   Y   N   P
19. Do you agree with Gandhi that a nation can be judged by how well its citizens care for animals?   Y   N   P
20. Do you agree that you should eat only what you are willing to kill?   Y   N   P

Your answers won't be graded right or wrong, but they should help you think about your own current spiritual beliefs and practices. The questions and the survey that follows are designed to help you know yourself better so you can become a better reconciler in the world around you.

You might also find it illuminating to share your answers with others you trust, and to listen to their responses. If you're reading this book with a group or if you're a member of a prayer or spirituality group, share these questions with the group and listen to each person's response. That alone will be an exercise in reconciliation, as you'll no doubt discover a wide variety of opinions expressed by individual group members.

How one understands self and community, especially in relationship to what I name as "nonviolent types," is also critical in learning to inhabit reconciliation. When we all see the world through our own lenses and press our perspective as the true and only one, we move away from inhabiting reconciliation. Instead, people and nations often move toward violence as a way of pressing their point or getting their own way. If we are to inhabit reconciliation, we must know what our own impulses are in terms of violence or nonviolence. This next survey will help you understand how you tend to see the world, as well as how others might view the exact same world.

Survey of Spiritual Types of Nonviolence

As best you can, spontaneously complete the following survey. Although there may be forced options, please circle the answer that comes closest to representing you. Your first inclination is the answer sought after in this survey.

Described are four patterns of spiritual types of nonviolence that may be used to assess your own style. Read across and circle the appropriate description that comes closest to your description of a spirituality of nonviolence. Please choose only one description in the pairing for each section.

Section A

I prefer to think of God's mercy.	or	I prefer to think of God's justice.
I am more open to the idea that God's love will eventually win over all of creation past, present, and future.	or	I am more open to the idea that God destroys evil and creates a new heaven and earth.
Peace, grace, contemplation, and restoration remind me more of God's presence.	or	Retribution, restitution, apocalypse, and prophecy remind me more of God's presence.
The Gospel requires me to practice grace and mercy in order to prove myself as neighbor and friend.	or	The Gospel requires me to practice right action toward my neighbor and friend.
Meditation and contemplation lead me to deeper understandings of forgiveness and reconciliation.	or	Meditation and contemplation lead me to deeper awareness of my adversaries.

Continue with Section B. Which person, word, or phrase in each across-the-page pairing appeals to you more? Think what the person means to you as well as what the word or phrase means, rather than how the word looks or how it sounds or the prestige of the person.

Section B

Dietrich Bonhoeffer	or	Gandhi
Malcolm X	or	Martin Luther King
Margaret Thatcher	or	Mother Teresa
Attachment	or	Detachment
Peter	or	John (the Beloved Disciple)
Theology	or	Mysticism

Continue this inventory of spiritual types by determining which pattern describes you best. Circle one phrase in each pairing that appeals to you most.

Section C

The church most needs saints.	or	The church most needs prophets.
I enjoy the mystery of thinking of God's peace beyond all understandings.	or	I enjoy thinking of the day when God will make all things new.
Sunday worship is my chief spiritual practice.	or	Centering prayer is my chief spiritual practice.
The Trinity is best understood as unity.	or	The Trinity is best understood as community.
"Come unto me all who labor . . . and I will give you rest."	or	"The truth shall set you free."

A final section follows. Continue the same practice of choosing one item from each coupling that appeals to you most.

Section D

Determined	or	Devoted
Will	or	Confession
Personal time in prayer is crucial to the spiritual life.	or	Communal worship is crucial to the spiritual life.
I must pay more attention to my journey with God.	or	I must seek a spiritual director.
Jesus died for me.	or	Jesus died for all.
Foresight	or	Compassion

Score Sheet

Count the number of descriptions you circled in the left column of Section A and add that number to the number of words and phrases you circled in the right column of Section B.
Write your total here: _____

Count the number of descriptions you circled in the right column of Section A and add that number to the number of words and phrases you circled in the left column of Section B.
Write your total here: _____

The sum of the two "totals" should be 11.

If the number in your first blank is a 6 or 7, circle: P-

If the number in your first blank is an 8 or 9, circle: P

If the number in your first blank is a 10 or 11, circle: P+

If the number in your first blank is 0 to 5, simply proceed with your scoring.

If the number in your second blank is a 6 or 7, circle: J-

If the number in your second blank is an 8 or 9, circle: J

If the number in your second blank is a 10 or 11, circle: J+

If the number in your second blank is 0 to 5, simply proceed with your scoring.

You should have either a P or J score, not one of each.

Next, count the number of sentences or words you circled in the left column of Section C and add that number to the number of items you circled in the right column of Section D.
Write that total here: _____

Next, count the number of sentences or words you circled in the right column of Section C and add that number to the number of items you circled in the left column of Section D.
Write that total here: _____

The sum of the two "totals" should be 11.

If the number in your first blank is a 6 or 7, circle: C-

If the number in your first blank is an 8 or 9, circle: C

If the number in your first blank is a 10 or 11, circle: C+

If the number in your first blank is 0 to 5, simply proceed with your scoring.

If the number in your second blank is a 6 or 7, circle: I-

If the number in your second blank is an 8 or 9, circle: I

If the number in your second blank is a 10 or 11, circle: I+

If the number in your second blank is 0 to 5, simply proceed with your scoring.

You should have either a C or an I score, not one of each.

Circle below the composite of the two letter scores you circled above.

P-/C-	P-/C	P-/C+	P-/I-	P-/I	P-/I+
P/C-	P/C	P/C+	P/I-	P/I	P/I+
P+/C-	P+/C	P+/C+	P+/I-	P+/I	P+/I+
J-/C-	J-/C	J-/C+	J-/I-	J-/I	J-/I+
J/C-	J/C	J/C+	J/I-	J/I	J/I+
J+/C-	J+/C	J+/C+	J+/I-	J+/I	J+/I+

On the following schema of "Spiritual Types of Nonviolence," there are two axes. The north-south scale is an "orientation/ends" scale. The upper hemisphere represents those who tend to seek more of a spirituality of community. Those in the southern hemisphere tend more toward a personal spirituality. The east-west scale is a "technique/means" scale, indicating preferred ways of going about a spirituality of nonviolence. Compare your questionnaire results with the explanation of letters (P, C, J, I) below. So, for example, if your composite score is P+/C+, you should move horizontally to the right along the P axis and then up into P and C quadrant. There you will find your description and characteristics. Plus or minus signs simply indicate levels of degree.

Spiritual Types of Nonviolence

Community (C)
Extreme = Communism

Retributive Spirituality (JC)
Social order
Utilitarian
Apocalyptic
Institutional

Restorative Spirituality (PC)
Social harmony
Utopian
Universalistic
Improvisational

Just Warrior (J)
Extreme = Civil Religion

Pacifist (P)
Extreme = Sectarian

Petrine Spirituality (JI)
Justice
Immediacy
Calculated Risk
Zealous

Johannine Spirituality (PI)
Mercy
Intermediacy
Blind Risk
Contemplative

Individual (I)
Extreme = Individualism

Assumptions and Implications

Before going into more detailed explanations of these approaches to reconciliation, I want to offer you some qualifications in order to empower your use of these typologies.

1. People tend to identify with one quadrant over another, but this by no means fixes personality types or worldviews.
2. Unless people live in tension with those in their opposing quadrant, they tend toward extremes. This is important to understand in the work of reconciliation, especially in learning to identify competing worldviews. So, instead of thinking in terms of competing types such as JC versus PI or PC versus JI, each type needs to learn to appreciate how an opposite type understands reconciliation. All quadrants need to stay in continuous tension to avoid extremes.
3. People tend to misunderstand those who identify with their opposite quadrant. Many of us aren't in the habit of looking at matters from someone else's perspective. Our first instinct is to do the opposite—to categorize opposing viewpoints as threats.
4. Instead of seeing people who think and act differently as immediate threats, I invite you to counter the instinctual urge to stereotype the other and instead understand that opposite worldviews can help you move toward balance and creativity.
5. Learning to live with different perspectives invites each of us to embrace a holistic spirituality. Wholeness is best understood in communal terms. No person is in all four quadrants (JC, PC, JI, and PI)—that's why communal spirituality is important.
6. Healthy communal spirituality is achieved in the affirmation and maintenance of all the quadrants and the management of the tensions among them.
7. A typical church is made up of people who identify with each of the quadrants. Unfortunately, members of the dominant group tend to insist that everyone be like them and members of minority groups tend to feel estranged. However, they need

each other, and the church needs all of them to affirm diverse perspectives and to minister to those caught up in a vortex of conflicting needs.

We can also investigate trends on a global scale. The communal-justice model (JC) is of increased interest in the economically developing world (e.g., Latin America, Africa). The individual-peace model (PI) is of increased interest in Western countries like the United States (e.g., the charismatic movement, Cursillo, personal Christian spirituality), especially among certain socioeconomic classes. There is also increased interest in the communal-peace model (PC); for example, in the growing movement of nonviolent protests in the Western world. At the same time, minorities (blacks, women, first Americans, Hispanics) are apt to be more interested in the individual-justice model (JI).

With all of this in mind, the following descriptions, each of them related to one of Jesus' parables, can help you understand your own as well as other people's approaches to conflict and reconciliation.

Community (C)

(JC)

- Goal: Immediate justice for all of creation
- Goodness of the law
- Vision for all of creation
- Common prayer
- Social protest
- Kingdom of God
- Extremes: Holy war, civil religion, survivalist group

(PC)

- Goal: Restoration of full communion with God
- Miracle of mercy
- Vision for the least of creation
- Daily Office of prayer
- Social resistance
- Kingdom of heaven
- Extreme: Quietism, apolitical, sectarian
- Parable: The Laborers in the Vineyard (Matthew 20:1–16)

Just (J)
Extreme = Fundamentalism

Peace (P)
Extreme = Quietism

(JI)

- Goal: Personal holiness
- Truth saying
- Parables: The Unfruitful Fig Tree (Luke 13:6–9); the Wedding Feast (Matthew 22:1–14)
- Prayer is petition
- Highest virtue: Courage
- Extreme: Fundamentalist

(PI)

- Goal: Personal peace
- Confession of sin
- Parables: The Laborers in the Vineyard (Matthew 20:1–16); the Lost Sheep (Matthew 18:12–14, Luke 15:1–7); the Lost Son (Luke 15:11–32)
- Prayer is contemplation
- Highest virtue: Humility
- Extreme: Pantheistic

Individual (I)

Typology for Communal Justice (JC)

- Goal: Immediate justice for all of creation
- Goodness of the law
- Vision for all of creation
- Common prayer
- Social protest
- Kingdom of God
- Extremes: Holy war, civil religion, survivalist
- Group parable: Unforgiving

Historical Characters: Early Zealots, confessional church, Mainline Protestants, the Vatican

Prayer: Common worship and prayer are Word and Eucharist centered

Spirituality: Active model (Martha, sister of Lazarus)

Liturgical Style: Ordered worship following set program, usually Sunday mornings

Goal: To engage in societal change through prophetic witness and socio-political-economic action

The communal justice typology can be found in Jesus' teaching moment with Peter and the subsequent parable of the Unforgiving Servant, both found in Matthew 18:21–35.

In the first story, Peter comes up to Jesus and asks: "Lord, how many times shall I forgive someone when one sins against me? Up to seven times?" Being a good rabbinical student, Peter knew to place the answer in his question. The answer was seven times—the number of completeness. But Jesus wanted to teach Peter that what we view as complete is not always as full as God's understanding of completion.

We often aim for what is complete "for me." Peter was seeing this way. He asked about a fellow church member who had sinned against him personally. Peter may have had an answer, but his question was wrong. Those caught up in Western individualism especially need to pay attention to Jesus here as he shocks Peter out of his individualistic world. In Peter's world, true reconciliation would always be defined by Peter's limited understanding of completion, as his number seven suggested. And completion wasn't just about Peter; it was about everyone.

The communal-justice model emphasizes not only what is best "for me," but "for us." Jesus answered, "Not seven times, but, I tell you, seventy-seven times," a colloquial phrase that meant an infinite, incalculable number. Peter needed to learn to imagine what was best not only for himself and for his own self-completion; he was pushed by Jesus to imagine beyond himself—for all of us. The biblical number for all of us is often represented by extrapolating numbers that go on and on—like grains of sand or stars in the sky—seventy-seven times.

Jesus goes on to teach about desiring justice for everyone with the parable told in Matthew 18:23–35. The kingdom of heaven is like a king who wanted to reconcile accounts with his servants, Jesus says. As the king began the reconciliation process, someone who owed him ten thousand talents was brought to him. According to custom, since the servant was not able to pay his debt, the king ordered that he and his wife and his children and all that he had be sold to repay the debt. The servant fell on his knees before him. "Have patience with me," he begged, "and I will pay you everything."

The king did an unusual thing for that time: he took pity on his servant, canceled the debt, and let him go. But when that servant went out, he came upon a fellow servant who owed him a hundred dollars. The servant grabbed the person and began to choke him. "Pay what you owe." the servant demanded. The second servant knelt and begged the first servant, "Have patience with me, and I will pay you." But the first servant refused, and instead had the second servant thrown into prison until the debt was repaid.

When the other servants saw what had happened, they were greatly distressed and went and told their master the king everything that had happened. Then the king called the servant in and said,

"You wicked slave! I forgave you all that debt because you pleaded with me. Should you not have had mercy on your fellow slave as I had mercy on you?" In anger, the king turned the first servant over to the jailers to be tortured until the debt was repaid in full.

Jesus then says something hard to understand for communal-peace (PC) nonviolent types like me. He says, "So my heavenly Father will also do to every one of you if you do not forgive your brother or sister from your heart." It is this push by Jesus to see that injustice will not be tolerated in the life of God that makes the communal-justice model work.

But remember, this is a parable, and in parables, literary devices like hyperbole and exaggeration are often used to make a point. I don't believe that Jesus intends to perpetuate cycles of violence in this parable by teaching that the first servant deserves to be tortured. I think Jesus is still teaching Peter, and thereby teaching us, that this parable points beyond the vicious world of kings and queens, slaves and masters. Jesus wants us to see beyond our own hypocrisy in demanding exact (complete) justice for others, while we in fact are never recipients of such cruel justice because of the mercy of God. In other words, we must learn like Peter that our number seven has to keep expanding.

Jesus invites each of us to feel and see the need for justice, but always through the lens of those who have been given mercy. In this paradox, communal justice is summed up as immediate justice needed for all of creation. This model of spirituality seeks what is in the best interest of the community rather than seeking only what is best for certain individuals. In such a context, retributive justice tends to make more sense, as those seeking communal justice seek to match the causes and effects of what is in the best interest of the community. An individual in this typology may even be willing to sacrifice his or her life for such immediate justice (e.g., volunteering for military service or expressing a public position on a very controversial point). Philosophically, those in this typology believe in a social order that resembles the utilitarian sensibility that the needs of the many always outweigh the needs of the few.

Those who tend to look through the lens of communal justice tend to look for the immediate reign of God in our midst. Perhaps this is so because such individuals are more likely to count the costs in following through with their understanding of justice and are willing even to die for the immediate outcome of what is in the best interest of the community. People like me, who gravitate more toward communal peace, must recognize, affirm, and understand the courage often found in communal-justice types.

A spirituality focused on communal justice leads to ordered forms of common worship and prayer and to the balanced Word and Eucharist in the community's gatherings. Communal spirituality also favors the active model, represented by Martha, sister of Lazarus. Martha was the one who actively cleaned and worked while her sister Mary contemplatively sat quietly at Jesus' feet (Luke 11:38–42). Throughout the history of Christian spirituality, the typologies of active and contemplative spirituality became known as representative of Martha (active spirituality) and Mary (contemplative spirituality). The constant witness of communal justice is active; it engages in societal change through prophetic witness and socio-political-economic action.

Individuals seeking communal justice intuitively know the need for human systems to protect and maintain what is good for the whole. Certain characteristics emerge from these institutional sensibilities: affinity for the goodness of the law, common prayer, social control, and the desire for the reign of God. Because of this affinity for institutionalism, the natural extremes for those in the communal-justice category are a tendency toward fundamentalism, holy war, civil religion, and survivalist religion as found in some cults. The person whose focus is on communal justice, therefore, needs to be in conversation with those who are focused on peace if he or she wants to avoid unhealthy extremes.

Typology for Communal Peace (PC)

- Goal: Restoration of full communion with God
- Miracle of mercy

- Vision for the least of creation
- Daily Office of prayer
- Social resistance
- Kingdom of heaven
- Extreme: Quietism, apolitical, sectarian
- Parable: The Laborers in the Vineyard (Matthew 20:1-16)

Historical Characters: Early monastics, Anabaptists, Quakers

Prayer: Forms of contemplation and meditation, silence, and Eucharist centered

Spirituality: Receptive model (Mary, sister of Lazarus)

Liturgical Style: Spiritual practices, daily worship

Goal: To engage in societal change through prayer and socio-political-economic witness and example

The communal-peace model focuses on restorative justice in contrast to the communal-justice model that emphasizes retributive justice. A famous example of someone demonstrating this type of spirituality is Archbishop Desmond Tutu.[1] People who tend toward communal peace seek social harmony as the ultimate end and therefore hold utopian visions for society. As a result, they are attracted to universal worldviews that encourage the goal of peace for all. Unlike the communal-justice model, those who advocate for communal peace are more likely to be improvisational instead of institutional.

The goal of those who gravitate toward the communal-peace model is the restoration of full communion with God. By seeking to love God with all of our hearts, souls, and bodies, we enter the mystery of not only loving God, but also our neighbor. Love for God cannot be separated from love of neighbor. Jesus was constantly asked about the great commandments of God's justice and law. And Jesus consistently pointed toward a restorative justice in which God's love co-mingles with the love of others. This means that God's love always points toward the peace and shalom of all of creation. And this is not just peace in the sense of the absence of war. Because of the mystery of God's love interpenetrating our love, peace has its own content apart from violence. God's peace is the proactive relationality that makes community and love intelligible.

Those who relate to the communal-peace model believe that peace needs communal preparation. We must prepare for peace through the Daily Office of prayer, as St. Benedict taught the monks in his abbey. Or we must prepare for peace by increasing the attention we give to those who suffer, as the Christian mystic Simone Weil taught.

Jesus' parable in Matthew 20:1–16 is one that teaches about the communal-peace perspective. The kingdom of heaven is like a landowner who went out early in the morning to hire laborers for a grape orchard. After agreeing with the laborers for the usual daily wage, the landowner sent them into the vineyard. When the landowner went out about nine o'clock in the morning and noticed others standing idle in a shopping center, he said to them, "You also go into the vineyard, and I will pay you whatever is right." So they went to work in the orchard.

When the owner went out again about noon and then about three o'clock, the same thing happened. And about five o'clock, the same thing happened again. "Why are you standing here idle all day?" he asked the laborers. The usual response was, "Because no one has hired us." Without fail, the owner would say to all of them, "You also go into the vineyard."

When evening came, the owner of the vineyard said to a manager, "Call the laborers and give them their pay, beginning with the last and then going to the first." When those hired at five o'clock came, each of them received the usual daily wage. Now when the first came, they thought they would receive more, but each of them also received the usual daily wage. And when they received it, they grumbled against the landowner, saying, "These last worked only one hour, and you have made them equal to us who have borne the burden of the day and the scorching heat." But the owner replied to one of them, "Friend, I am doing you no wrong; did you not agree with me for the usual daily wage? Take what belongs to you and go; I choose to give to this last the same as I give to you. Am I not allowed to do what I choose with what belongs to me? Or are you envious because I am generous? So the last will be first, and the first will be last."

In this parable, Jesus tries to get us to think beyond our individual concepts of retributive justice and begin to imagine God (the owner) and the utopian vision that results from the way in which God operates in the world. God does not operate with us through hierarchy, as the later workers in the vineyard seemed to desire. Rather, God operates based on generosity and on gift giving. That kind of perspective proved difficult for many disciples to understand, including one of Jesus' best friends, Martha. Martha wanted her sister, Mary, to get up and earn the right to be in Jesus' presence. So Martha tried to model this work in the vineyard herself. Unlike Martha's active model of spirituality, communal-peace people tend toward a spirituality seen through the contemplative model represented by Mary, the sister of Lazarus.

Those who tend toward communal peace may favor more of a liturgical style that includes contemplative spiritual practices such as centering prayer and *lectio divina*. Daily worship also becomes a necessary discipline. The main prayer techniques tend to include forms of contemplation and meditation, silence, and Eucharist-centered community. Work with prisoners or those on death row would be typical of those who represent communal peace, since they gravitate toward the generosity of God and God's intent to restore all of creation. No individual is to be deemed worthless or idle. Those who could be seen in this communal-peace category are the early monastics, Anabaptists, Christian peace fellowships, and Quakers. Their ultimate goal is to engage God's infinite generosity and restoration through societal change, prayer, and socio-political-economic witness and example.

The extreme danger for those in this category is their tendency toward quietism or apolitical stances in which God's ultimate peace is seen as having no relevance to structural and institutional involvement. Another possible extreme is the adherents' tendency toward sectarian division, adopting an "us against the world" mentality. Instead of such extremes, the balance between individual engagement and communal-justice engagement becomes crucial for seekers of communal peace to reach their goal.

Typology for Individual Justice (JI)

- Goal: Personal holiness
- Truth saying
- Parables: The Unfruitful Fig Tree (Luke 13:6–9); the Wedding Feast (Matthew 22:1–14)
- Prayer is petition
- Highest virtue: Courage
- Extreme: Fundamentalist

Historical Characters: Peter, Martin Luther, Dietrich Bonhoeffer

Prayer: Forms of confession, forgiveness, repentance

Spirituality: Active model (Martha, sister of Lazarus)

Liturgical Style: Ordered worship

Goal: To engage in societal change through socio-political-economic action

A spirituality of individual justice revolves around immediate justice, a calculated outcome for one's own deeds and misdeeds, and passion for a cause. These are the same characteristics seen in the communal-justice model, but personalized. We see the individual-justice model in some of the conversations and teachings between Jesus and Peter. Peter felt very passionately about Jesus and what he believed. Christians often forget this about Peter—that he was willing to die violently by taking on the Roman guards. Another example of Peter's individual determination toward justice can be seen in Peter's assertion that he of all the disciples would never abandon Jesus (Matthew 26:33). The goal of this spiritual model is personal holiness.

Some of the parables of Jesus that categorize individual justice are the Unfruitful Fig Tree (Luke 13:6-9) and the Wedding Feast (Matthew 22:1-14). I'll focus on the latter to illustrate the model. Jesus said:

> The kingdom of heaven may be compared to a king who gave a wedding banquet for his son. He sent his slaves to call those who had been invited to the wedding banquet, but they would not come. Again he sent other slaves, saying, "Tell those who have been invited: Look, I have prepared my dinner, my oxen and my fat calves have been slaughtered, and everything is ready; come to the wedding banquet." But they made light of it and went away, one to his farm, another to his business, while the rest seized his slaves, mistreated them, and killed them. The king was enraged. He sent his troops, destroyed those murderers, and burned their city. Then he said to his slaves, "The wedding is ready, but those invited were not worthy. Go therefore into the main streets, and invite everyone you find to the wedding banquet." Those slaves went out into the streets and gathered all whom they found, both good and bad; so the wedding hall was filled with guests.
>
> But when the king came in to see the guests, he noticed a man there who was not wearing a wedding robe, and he said to him, "Friend, how did you get in here without a wedding robe?" And he was speechless. Then the king said to the attendants, "Bind him hand and foot, and throw him into the outer darkness, where there will be weeping and gnashing of teeth." For many are called, but few are chosen.

How does this parable relate to individual justice? In short, Jesus again uses hyperbole to exaggerate the circumstance in which a student of spirituality may learn how to respond to a harsh world of kings and violent systems. Usually, in such a world, the highest virtue achieved by individual justice is courage. Jesus, however, creatively teaches through this parable that resistance to the king (killing his servants and boldly rejecting the king's invitations) were not signs of courage, but foolishness. It seems to me that the crucial point of this parable is the determination of individual justice. But such a determination is awfully risky, because, as I said earlier, one's own perspective often gets in the way. I think this is why the parable continues. The individual is thrown into darkness, thereby making the lost individual the focal point of justice because he lacked wisdom in engaging those at the wedding. He resembles Peter, who thought so many times that his example alone would set matters straight. The burden of those who follow the individual-justice model is in making connections to other worldviews and perspectives. Because, after all, which justice and whose justice are we talking about? As Nelson Mandela illustrates through his own biography, one person's "terrorist" can eventually become another person's "freedom fighter" or even "the greatest President" in human history. People who identify with the spiritual model of individual justice share Peter's sensibilities. Their ultimate goal is to personally engage in societal change through socio-political-economic action. Their spirituality is more like the active model, in which Martha burdened herself with housework as a way of providing hospitality for Jesus while her sister Mary sat contemplatively at Jesus' feet, doing nothing to help. Like Martha, those following the individual-justice model personally vow that if no one else in the world demonstrates justice, they at least will show justice in their own lives.

In such a spirituality, the primary understanding of prayer tends to be through individual petitions for certain causes, issues, or persons. Another natural form of prayer includes the rite of reconciliation in which the practices of confession, forgiveness, and repentance increasingly become vitally important in one's personal life. A natural liturgical style for this model of individual justice would be personal worship in which one is personally nourished. Some historical characters that may represent this model of individual justice are Peter, Martin Luther, and Dietrich

Bonhoeffer. What those who see through a lens of individual justice need to be mindful of is the possibility of the extremes of
becoming isolated, individualistic, and a fundamentalist.

Typology for Individual Peace (PI)

- Goal: Personal peace
- Confession of sin
- Parables: The Laborers in the Vineyard (Matthew 20:1–16);
  the Lost Sheep (Matthew 18:12–14, Luke 15:1–7); the Lost
  Son (Luke 15:11–32)
- Prayer is contemplation
- Highest virtue: Humility
- Extreme: Pantheistic

Historical Characters: St. John, St. Francis, and Mother Teresa

Prayer: Forms of contemplation

Spirituality: Receptive model (Mary, Sister of Lazarus)

Liturgical Style: Sacramental

Goal: To engage in societal change through prayer and socio-political-
economic witness and example

I see this last model of spirituality best represented by the Beloved
Disciple described in the Gospels as the disciple John. More specifi-
cally, in John's gospel we see the Mary-like tendency in John to rest
contemplatively in Jesus' presence (see John 21:20–24). Johannine
spirituality tends toward such individual rest or peace. Its chief
characteristics are: mercy, personal intermediacy, and contemplation. Besides Johannine materials in the Bible, the parables of Jesus
that tend toward individual peace are: the Lost Sheep (Matthew
18:12–14; Luke 15:1–7) and the Prodigal Son (Luke 15:11–32).

Indeed, one of the best ways to describe this model is through Jesus' parable of the Prodigal Son, to which we now turn.

Jesus tells a story about the younger brother leaving home. According to the Jewish law of the day, the share of the younger of two sons would be a third of the father's estate. The young son not only wants his share of the estate turned into hard currency, but he also wants what many young people want—adventure and independence. His fault, therefore, is not in his desire to leave home, but in the squandering of resources. After all, "prodigal" means reckless or extravagant.

The reckless youth soon spends his inheritance. In Luke 15:15 we discover the depth of the tragedy, and witness a wealthy young man begging from unclean animals. This eating with pigs implies that the youth had not only lost his material resources, but had also lost his spirituality—doing the unthinkable for a Jew, sharing food with pigs.

Then the young man "comes to himself" in verses 17–19. In other words, he comes to his senses and realizes the tragedy of it all. This recognition is driven primarily by the peaceful memory of his loving father. This "coming to himself" is not about repentance or conversion at this stage; rather, it is the surprise of the young man seeing himself as he truly is. The young man returns home.

The father emerges to take a lead role in the parable (verses 20–24). He runs out to meet his son in what is a very undignified way for an Oriental elder. But this is an exceptional man, surprised by his son's return. The father runs to his son before the son can even acknowledge his guilt. In a sense, they both become prodigals, as both display uncontrolled joy toward one another. What was lost is now found. This rediscovery of peace and joy becomes a key theme in many of Jesus' parables, especially in the Gospel of Luke.

The genius of the parable is in the surprise of mutual initiative by the son and the father. Both of their actions speak louder than words. The garments, signet ring, and shoes speak of the father's reinstatement of the prodigal son into the family, as does the father's own prodigal behavior of lavishing wealth on an undeserving son.

Then a joyous feast occurs, for the father's son has come back to life; he was lost and is found. The parable would appear to end here, but it does not. The elder son takes center stage.

The parable becomes a diptych in which the elder son ultimately becomes the focus of the parable, which is more concerned with the fault of the elder son than that of the younger son. The elder son's sense of justice vehemently protests a love that seems to confound all sense of values. He is not so much upset by the feast or the calf or the meal as by the behavior of the father: this inconceivable love. He does not even address his father as "Father." Nor will he call the prodigal brother his brother; rather, he is merely a "son of yours!" But the father still speaks of the reality of the relationship as he addresses the elder son as *teknon,* "my dear child," and gently reminds him of who it is that has come back: "[T]his brother of yours was dead and has come to life; he was lost and has been found"—it is right to celebrate his resurrection. But all of this seems absurd and outrageous to the elder son, who cannot see what is motivating his father or how he can be so happy. Now it is the elder son, not the prodigal, who is in danger of becoming lost.[2]

What the younger son and the father teach us to see is the goal of personal peace. There is an increasing repertoire of spiritual practices for those adopting individual-peace spirituality. Among their chief spiritual practices are centering prayer, silence, humility, transcendental meditation, yoga. Their highest virtue is humility. Their chief forms of prayer are naturally contemplative. The receptive model of Mary, sister of Martha, describes those who identify with individual peace and who would rather simply be in the presence of God. A favored liturgical style would look like Taizé worship, a form of contemplative chanting and silence. Those who see through the lens of individual peace appreciate liturgical styles that emphasize sacramental presence. The ultimate goal is to engage in societal change through personal prayer and individual socio-political-economic witness and example.

The extreme of those in the individual-peace category is that absolutes and reality merge as individuals seek their own inner peace. If one is not careful, truth becomes relativistic if not anarchic.

Reality is seen only through the individual perspective. But what happens when individual realities bump up against each other?

The Balance of the Four Types

Keep in mind that people tend to identify with one quadrant over another, but this by no means fixes personality types or world-views. Unless people live in tension with their opposing quadrant, they tend toward extremism. For example, those who find themselves in the category of communal justice (JC) must learn to relate to those in the individual-peace (PI) category. As the axiom goes: There can be no peace without justice. And so it is with the opposing quadrants of communal peace (PC) and individual justice (JI). Overall peace requires the effort of every individual. So, instead of have competing types such as JC versus PI or PC versus JI, it is my hope that each type can learn to appreciate the other, thereby broadening each one's understanding of reconciliation. Therefore, all quadrants should stay in continuous tension to avoid extremes.

The goal of discussing the differences described in each quadrant is to move toward understanding differences rather than just tolerating them. In other words, instead of merely settling for tolerating others, our goal is to learn to understand the other—and even more, to need the other. Such understanding and need inevitably lead to fuller relationships and to the lessening of inadvertent offense and full-blown war.

CHAPTER 3
Inhabiting Reconciliation

Maybe you've seen the church bloopers that have circulated on the Internet over the years. They're usually misprints from church newsletters or bulletins, statements like: "Don't let worry kill you off—let the Church help." One that circulates regularly highlights both the need for reconciliation and our perpetual challenge with it. "The peacemaking meeting scheduled for today," it reads, "has been cancelled due to conflict." That's funny and makes us chuckle, but it also reminds us of the uncomfortable truth that we will always be in need of restorative practices to help mend broken personal, communal, and global relationships. We are constantly challenged to inhabit reconciliation.

That sounds pessimistic, but that's not my intention. It's hard to deny that each of us acts on destructive tendencies, at least on occasion. Working through the typologies in the previous chapter has probably reminded you of more than one conflict in your life. Part of what makes the above church blooper funny is that it's easy to imagine a church committee being contentious and not wanting to see each other. And the morning newspaper and the evening news are packed with stories of enough pain and evil to make anyone weep.

But we are equally capable of inhabiting goodness and flourishing. And that is true because God already inhabits us. God has already reconciled us. Paul explains, "So if anyone is in Christ, there is a new creation: everything old has passed away; see, everything has become new! All this is from God, who [has already] reconciled us to himself through Christ, and has given us the ministry of reconciliation" (2 Corinthians 5:17–18). Paul speaks in the past tense: God has already reconciled us through Christ. Our task is to practice the presence of Christ and live (inhabit) such divine life, not as some utopian vision but as concrete reality.

But living that way—inhabiting reconciliation—continues to be challenging at best and excruciatingly painful at worst, even for committed Christians. Witness the difficulty many denominations experience over issues of sexuality. Richard Mouw, philosopher and seminary president of Fuller Theological Seminary, in a recent article describes the pain we cause one another:

> The issues that we are discussing are not simply topics about which we happen to disagree. They are matters that are vitally connected to the question of whether we can stay together as a denomination. In that sense, our present Presbyterian debates do not feel like friendly arguments over the breakfast table, or even the more heated kinds of exchanges that might take place in the presence of a marriage counselor. Rather, it often feels like we are already getting ready for the divorce court, under pressure to measure every word that we say with an eye toward the briefs that our lawyers will be presenting as we move toward a final settlement.[1]

Mouw's insight is not just for the Presbyterians, but also for all who call themselves Christians. Each of us needs to practice, not just talk about, reconciliation. Reconciliation is the whole-hearted process of yielding negative conflict in exchange for God's positive outcome.[2] That yielding of negative conflict is that concrete practice of reconciliation I so long for.

Yielding the Negative

Yielding negative feelings, practicing reconciliation, is tough work. Most of us know from personal experience how difficult it is to let go of angry or hurt feelings. Perhaps that's why people who demonstrate this ability impress us so much. On the evangelical campus of Calvin College, scholar Virginia Mollenkott "came out" and told people about her sexual orientation as a lesbian: "You may disagree with everything I have said thus far," Mollenkott lectured, "but I hope we can at least agree on this: whatever your sexual orientation, there is nothing—absolutely nothing—that you have to do or agree to before coming to the foot of the cross of Jesus. The only thing any of us has to say as we come to Calvary is this: 'Just as I am without one plea, but that thy blood was shed for me, and that thou bidst me come to thee, O Lamb of God, I come.'"[3] Mollenkott yielded the negative, and invited her audience to see what they had in common. She invited them to inhabit God's positive outcome with her.

In her book *Women Who Run with the Wolves*,[4] Clarissa Pinkola Estés also encourages a yielding of negative conflict that can be released properly in anger, but she warns against getting stuck in it. The energy that rage demands can be used in positive ways, but the allure of using it for destruction is usually more seductive. Estés suggests a process of inviting anger to take a seat, have tea with us, and talk a while so we can find out what summoned this visitor. Recognize, bless, contain, and then release the anger, she recommends. Releasing the anger isn't about overlooking our pain or the wrong done to us, but about becoming agile and strong and detaching ourselves from destructive tendencies that invite us into the quicksand of violence.

All of this takes practice. Just as people have to learn to weave, to write, to do carpentry, each of us needs to learn how to be reconciling and then to practice those skills. Inhabiting reconciliation involves learning to create space between you and whatever hurts. Practicing these skills and accepting the grace of God lead to life and a future. They lead to inhabiting God.

Some people believe that they've done nothing to deserve God's love. They shy away from practices of reconciliation and other experiences that might end—they fear—in discovering just how little God cares for them. But St. Teresa of Avila speaks of God's love as a drenching spring rain—something that covers everything. In response to that drenching, many of us experience utter gratitude as well as profound sorrow and desolation when we realize how careless and indifferent we can be to God's love. Instead of remaining guilty and forlorn, God's love invites our habitation, as Anglican poet and priest George Herbert so beautifully describes:

> Love bade me welcome, yet my soul drew back,
>   Guilty of dust and sin.
> But quick-ey'd Love, observing me grow slack
>   From my first entrance in,
> Drew nearer to me, sweetly questioning
>   If I lack'd anything.
>
> "A guest," I answer'd, "worthy to be here";
>   Love said, "You shall be he."
> "I, the unkind, the ungrateful? ah my dear,
>   I cannot look on thee."
> Love took my hand and smiling did reply,
>   "Who made the eyes but I?"
>
> "Truth, Lord, but I have marr'd them; let my shame
>   Go where it doth deserve."
> "And know you not," says Love, "who bore the blame?"
>   "My dear, then I will serve."
> "You must sit down," says Love, "and taste my meat."
>   So I did sit and eat.[5]

Love, as we learn to embrace it, leads us toward the banquet of reconciliation. And that banquet isn't a passive event; it invites active participation. Accepting God's love and choosing to inhabit reconciliation means that we commit ourselves to learning to anticipate conflicts and opt to seek solutions rather than further the pain or hurt.

This isn't just a simple, pretty, and idealistic statement. When Archbishop Tutu led the Truth and Reconciliation Commission in South Africa after the end of apartheid, the stories and atrocities revealed in those meetings brought enormous pain to the attention of the nation as a whole. There was nothing pretty or idealistic about it. But it was also reconciling. It was action, not pretty words, which led to reconciliation. As Christians, we believe through our practices. Belief without action, without practice, isn't real belief. And our practice of reconciliation invites others to practice inhabiting reconciliation as well. Such inhabiting emulates the atmosphere of God, whose community of persons (Father, Son, and Holy Spirit) creates out of nothing, *ex nihilo*; or, to put it another way, it mimics God's ways, always opting to create rather than to destroy. God's creation of us invites us into such divine life. We cannot help but be wrapped up in God. Reconciliation is our participation in the act of creation, and there are as many ways to do it as there are people.

My work in this book is to show you what inhabiting reconciliation looks like—with skin on, as the little boy in the joke in Chapter 1 said. Pictures of reconciliation guard against the despair that seeks to define existence. With all the violence that finds its way to our attention, stories of reconciliation are the hope we need to hang on to. There are five steps in the process of reconciliation. Two of them (contrition and confession) are ones in which we can engage for ourselves. The remaining three (repentance, forgiveness, and reunion) are the gifts of God.

From Contrition to Reunion

Reconciliation isn't a pill we can take; it's a process we have to learn. The most basic elements of this process of reconciliation are: contrition, confession, forgiveness, repentance, and finally, reunion. Although I'm presenting this in a linear fashion, in reality we move in and out of these five areas rather than going through them consecutively.

Contrition

"What should I do about my sins?" asked the monk of the desert saint Anthony. "Whoever seeks deliverance from sins will find it in tears and weeping," Anthony replied, "and whoever wishes to advance in building up virtue will do so through weeping and tears." Contrition is that recognition of one's own sins and the sorrow we feel for having committed them. The Greeks named this experience *penthos*, an affective movement of the heart, pierced with sorrow, groaning, and finally turning anew to God.

The process of reconciliation is about accepting our own sinfulness, about being contrite. Admitting our sinfulness, however, can be the most difficult part of the process. This is especially true in an individualistic society that likes to blame others for the harm we ourselves have done. But as Christians, we are asked to see ourselves more clearly and admit our sinfulness. This isn't about demeaning or belittling ourselves. We're not invited to hate ourselves or to hate others who sin. True contrition isn't about self-pity or ego-centered guilt. Contrition is simply the awareness of a truth about ourselves, that we are sinful beings, and ignoring that fact is risky business.

As members of Christian communities, we are also invited to commit ourselves again and again to the communal dimensions of what contrition can do for us. True contrition is a community affair that leads to forgiveness of self and others. Contrition requires that a person be capable of recognizing certain thoughts and behaviors as painful and harmful to self and community. The contrite person also recognizes how his or her sinful thoughts and actions are more than careless mistakes. A truly contrite person seeks to move away from sinfulness. In short, contrition is the ability to see a harmful pattern emerging in self and community. Before there can be constructive confession, there must be contrition, the healthy formation of human conscience from which to declare or confess the truth about harmful behaviors.

Confession

The second element in the process of reconciliation, confession, is the articulation of remorse. Such articulation does more than just notice the harm done. Speaking about it is a conscious witness and accounting for the harm done to self and others. Whereas contrition is primarily an emotional experience, confession is composed of emotion and resolve mixed together; confession is the conscious commitment to move away from harmful patterns.

Confession takes on two forms: communal and personal confessions. Personal confession, historically, involved confessing to a priest or another mediator, sometimes a monk or a nun. In recent years, many churches have focused less on this practice (especially Protestant churches) and they sanction instead the confessions that occur between an individual and God. The balance for personal confession has increased, however, through communal confession, which often takes place in the liturgies of the prayer life of a community.

Ritual is a powerful way to nurture both private and communal confessions, but this may be an arena of great failure today. Few Protestant churches inform parishioners about the practice of personal confession or offer it to them. The Roman Catholic Church has also seen a decline in the number of parishioners who come for personal confession. The situation in worship is no better. For many worshipers, ritual gestures of confession have become routine and empty. The practice no longer moves them to a profound sense of loss and mourning. Every week in many churches we are made aware of violence and indifference to human beings through our confession of sin. Can we, however, bring these sinful realities to their fullest light so that the ritual arouses in the community the truest articulation of the prayer "Most merciful God, we confess that we have sinned against you"?

The work of Susan Vanzanten Gallagher is helpful in further
illustrating what I mean by the need to articulate confession.[6]
Gallagher analyzed the confessional mode in what has become the
most famous case of reconciliation, South Africa's Truth and
Reconciliation Commission led by Archbishop Desmond Tutu.
The rise of the protest poem, the contemporary praise-song, the
township drama, and the prison memoir become major examples
of reconciliation in South African literature. South Africa's example
of articulating sins, injustices, and oppression proves to be important in light of those who are highly skeptical of the possibility of
reconciliation.

South Africa's Truth and Reconciliation hearings of the 1990s
produced confessional literature that has carved out a new national
identity based on geography rather than race. Such a move was a
stroke of genius and God's grace. Public confessional literature,
especially that which is autobiographical in nature, illustrates confessional ways of knowing. Gallagher wisely acknowledges that the
confessional mode in South African literature is not a good in and
of itself. Pseudo-confessions or narcissistic confessions are also rife
in such discourse. However, confession that understands and
acknowledges a debt enables people to construct notions of a self
(even of a new nation) through narrative that is wary of those who
make destructive claims on the truth. Ultimately, confession is the
speech that leads to the actions that facilitate human flourishing
rather than oppression and destruction.

Forgiveness

The third element of reconciliation is forgiveness. Forgiveness is
the deliberate opening of ourselves to that which heals and
restores us and the refusal to let harm define our lives. To forgive
requires real strength; it is heroic. Nelson Mandela, the South
African leader who was jailed for many years under what was then
known in South Africa as the "Terrorist Act," is a perfect example
of someone in whom forgiveness is strength instead of weakness.

Unfortunately, we can't make forgiveness happen. It is a gift of God. But it is a gift we can be open to receiving. Practices such as yielding what is negative, consciously resisting what is negative, and giving it to God will help us be open to receiving the gift of forgiveness.

Perhaps paradoxically, forgiveness of others also frees us from the control of the one who injured us. Our own anger holds us prisoner. "If you forgive the sins of any," Jesus tells us, "they are forgiven them; if you retain the sins of any, they are retained" (John 20:23). Jesus gives the disciples the insight that forgiveness can free us, or if lacking forgiveness, they may enslave us. Forgiveness is that powerful, supernatural act of breaking the abusive cycles of violence that imprison us and others.[7]

Repentance

Repentance is the fourth element in the process of reconciliation, one that deepens the act of forgiveness. A repentant person continues the supernatural work of forgiveness by restoring, as best he or she can, any damage done. We can't make repentance happen; it is the natural outcome of our working on the first three parts of the reconciliation process. Repentance is the visible manifestation of the changes we make in the process of contrition, confession, and forgiveness. Robert Enright, a developmental psychologist at the University of Wisconsin, has formed the International Forgiveness Institute to explore issues of emotional and physical healing that can result from reconciliation. Enright believes that those who practice reconciliation experience a reduction in psychological depression and are more quickly restored to wellness.

Reunion

The fifth and last element in the process of reconciliation is reunion—a step that is often lost or unrecognized in our thinking about reconciliation. Reunion involves embracing the offender—

kissing and embracing the prodigal son—something seldom seen (or rarely authentic). Reunion may scare most of us more than any other step in the process. But we must remember, reunion is God's ultimate gift and hope for us. The work of reconciliation prepares us to receive that gift—even to recognize such a gift.

These five elements make up the reconciliation God offers to the world. Unless we practice living in this atmosphere of reconciliation, the gift of reunion will be too painful for us. Without adapting to God's ways of reconciliation, we won't be able to breathe in the atmosphere of God. And without adapting to God's ways, reunion to many only becomes the perversion of justice or some unearned conclusion. In the end, the inhabitation of reconciliation exemplified by Jesus takes us beyond the atmosphere of a violent world back into the intention of God's life for all of us. This is why the final step is called "reunion" instead of "union." God has always desired to be reunited with us, ever since Adam and Eve left the garden of Eden. Christian reconciliation offers this reunion in an atmosphere in which we all can live and even flourish.

CHAPTER 4
Crossing the Threshold of Reconciliation

O God, you are my God; I seek you;
my soul thirsts for you; my flesh faints for you,
as in a dry and weary land where there is no water.

—Psalm 63:1

The scene is a familiar one today. A child sits in front of the television watching an afternoon cartoon or playing a video game. His entire body and mind are focused on the activity, as if nothing else existed. His mom comes into the room and asks him if he's done his homework or tells him that dinner is ready. No response. The boy doesn't even hear his mother. The atmosphere with which he has surrounded himself is whatever fiction is on the television or embedded in the video game. That's his reality. That's what holds his focus. Whatever else may be going on in the room, the house, the neighborhood, or anywhere else is inconsequential.

Children aren't the only ones who focus their attention this way. Adults, too, sit for hours in front of the television. Both adults and children spend hours in front of computer screens, surfing the net. For good or for bad, technology has become a focal point in our culture, one that often takes us away from more interactive and communal focuses. We're concentrating on something that demands very little from us. It's easier to zap something in the microwave or pick up a prepared dinner on the way home from work and let the family sit in front of the television for dinner than it is to plan a meal, shop for the food, cook it, and take the time to sit down together and talk.

The merits (and demerits) of this kind of living has been explored by sociologists, psychologists, and others, and will continue to be discussed for years to come. My concern isn't about whether these lifestyle tendencies are good or evil in and of themselves; this isn't the place to argue that. But it is clear that, as a culture, we've put things such as television viewing, video games, and other activities that require little from us at the center of our lives. We're becoming accustomed to being passive, to skipping activities that ask effort or commitment from us. Reconciliation—which is hard work, hard work that is active and that threatens to challenge and change our worldviews—seems too difficult to many people. It's easier just to stay in the house, turn on the television or the computer, and let the world present itself to us in ways that don't require a response.

The rewards, however, of sitting passively in front of the TV are proportional to the effort put in. The same is true of the rewards of inhabiting reconciliation. If we are going to be reconciling people, we must find ways to make reconciliation part of the atmosphere in which we live in much the same way that television, video games, and fast food become part of the reality of many people's lives. We have to seek reconciliation, just as the psalmist quoted at the beginning of this chapter seeks God. "O God, you are my God; I seek you; my soul thirsts for you; my flesh faints for you" (Psalm 63:1).

But to do that will be countercultural. Albert Borgmann, Regents Professor of Philosophy at the University of Montana, explains why. In an interview published in 2003 in *The Christian Century*, Borgman explored his own research on technology and its effect on culture today: Do we control technology or does technology control us?[1] Borgmann concludes that technology has the upper hand right now. With less effort on our parts than ever before (we don't even have to get up to change the channel on the television anymore), technology takes care of all our needs and provides increasingly high levels of comfort. We don't have to interact with one another or with the objects in our world very much. And that technology is so pervasive today that few people can resist its allure.

Consequently, people today spend more time doing solitary activities—watching TV, working or playing on a computer, grabbing a quick meal from a fast-food place—and less time interacting with others. This has become the atmosphere in which most of us live today. No longer do storytelling, reading, spending time in silence, and engaging in activities that nurture friendships take up much of our time. Reconciliation, a communal activity, is another thing that slips off the radar screen in a society that discourages community.

Borgmann doesn't blame technology for the problem. We are the source of the difficulty. But we have allowed ourselves to be mesmerized into thinking of technology as the solution to every problem or concern. We mistakenly believe that technology, not people, should feed the starving and heal the sick. Borgmann believes that the inducements of a technological culture have imperceptibly moved to colonize individualistic worldviews in the Western world. The notion that the individual alone is the best judge of what constitutes the good life makes it difficult for most of us to imagine what the common or collective good life might be. Today's individualism makes it hard to imagine that others would desire reconciliation, much less conceive what use the church could be as a reconciling force in a violent world.

What those of us who want to be reconciling individuals must do is resist the allure of individualistic thinking. In a very real way, getting out from behind the television or computer screen and having dinner with the family or going to play tennis with a friend is a step toward our becoming reconciling persons. We need to learn to place reasonable boundaries around our individual desires and to seek to create a society and a church that looks out for the good of the whole. We need to engage in activities that ask more of us than do television and computer games. If television is the focal point in our lives and we never ask more of ourselves than the effort required to watch television, we won't be able to develop the skills we need to become reconcilers.

Borgmann speaks of thresholds and the amount of effort it takes to cross one. The greater the amount of effort required, the greater the reward. Watching television or playing video games requires very little effort and offers little in the way of rewards. High-threshold activities are the ones we need to engage in. You don't have to exert yourself physically or face danger for the threshold to be considered high; sitting down to a communal meal is an example of an activity that has a high threshold. But the high threshold does demand more effort from us. Eating with the family requires more attention and focus than eating alone in front of the television set. But the reward, for our souls, is proportional to the effort put in.

Jesus says: "But love your enemies, do good, and lend, expecting nothing in return. Your reward will be great, and you will be children of the Most High" (Luke 6:35). In an individualistic culture, that doesn't look like much of a reward for lending and expecting nothing in return. We want interest on what we've lent. Jesus teaches, however, that until we learn to seek the higher rewards— the ones that include everyone, rather than just one person—that no one is truly rewarded. Jesus invites us to cross the highest thresholds, the ones that result in the common good, rather than wrapping ourselves up in momentary comfort or distraction.

Reconciliation asks us to change our focal point in the same way, from an individualistic focus to one that champions the common good. Obviously, we're not being socialized to do that. Even much of Christian spirituality today speaks to the individual without concern for the community. What is required of those of us who want to be reconcilers is attention to the community as a whole and a spirituality that is active, practical, and tangible. As Mother Teresa said, "Give them Jesus."

This requires effort. We can't be reconcilers or facilitate reconciliation in our homes and communities and world without learning the practices and living them first for ourselves. But the rewards for recognizing this and for becoming reconcilers are three. First, we will discover how extraordinary what we are doing—particularly in church—really is. Instead of watching television, we decide to practice the presence of God, and we begin to see how amazing worship really is. Our gatherings become filled with grace in a way we didn't recognize before. Second, we can become leaders in reshaping the focal points in our own culture today. We can become proponents for nonviolence instead of war and for equal distribution of wealth and resources. Finally, as people who open themselves to the world at large, we begin to understand ourselves as the lifelong students of God. We learn humility. And when all these things come together—an intelligent understanding of the patterns of contemporary society and confidence in God as a part of the very atmosphere in which we live and breathe—then we can hope that we are one step closer to the kingdom of God.

Expanding Vision: A Contemporary Parable

As we work on shifting our focal point from the creature comforts of our lives to the world around us, one of the first things we begin to learn is that we cannot define God and that God can reconcile the world beyond what we can possibly imagine, certainly beyond the systems and rules we have set up. God proves this repeatedly in stories and parables from the Bible.

Consider this story, a contemporary parable:

> The water of life, wishing to make itself known on the face of the earth, bubbled up in an artesian well and flowed without effort or limit. People came to drink of the magic water and were nourished by it, since it was so clean and pure and invigorating. But humankind was not content to leave things in this Edenic state. Gradually they began to fence the well, charge admission, claim ownership of the property around it, make elaborate laws as to who could come to the well, put locks on the gates. Soon the well was the property of the powerful and the elite. The water was

angry and offended; it stopped flowing and began to bub-
ble up in another place. The people who owned the property around the first well were so engrossed in their power
systems and ownership that they did not notice that the
water had vanished. *They continued to sell the tap water as if
it were the water of life,* and few people noticed that the true
power was gone. But some dissatisfied people searched
with great courage and found the new artesian well. Soon
that well was under the control of the property owners,
and the same fate overtook it. The spring took itself to yet
another place—and this has been going on throughout
recorded history.[2]

The community in this parable tried to control life, much in the
same way that the church often tries to control the Spirit. The community's deepest sorrow was its inability to keep up with what the
living water was doing. They wanted control over it, so much so
that they kept selling tap water as if it were the same thing as the
water of life. This is the same lesson Jesus teaches the disciples.
Repeatedly he invited them to stop practicing shallow forms of
piety and practice living into the most profound relationship
between God and humanity. That kind of relationship required
that the disciples relinquish their understandings of what God
could or could not do.

The prophet Amos tried to teach the same thing. Amos tried to
get the people to stop limiting the justice of God: "Seek the LORD
and live, or he will break out against the house of Joseph like fire,
and it will devour Bethel, with no one to quench it. Ah, you that
turn justice to wormwood, and bring righteousness to the ground!"
(Amos 5:6–7). The psalmist also tries to get us to see that we cannot define the ways of God, that God is the one who defines us.

Before the mountains were brought forth,
   or the land and the earth were born,
      from age to age you are God.

You turn us back to the dust and say,*
"Go back, O child of earth."

For a thousand years in your sight are like yesterday
when it is past*
and like a watch in the night.

(Psalm 90:2–4, BCP)

What Jesus teaches us through parables is the goal of Christian spirituality—not to define God, but to allow God to define—for us to learn to inhabit fully God's life. Our work of reconciliation is the same work, that of expanding our vision to see how God reconciles the world in ways we haven't imagined or legislated.

If this seems difficult to learn or remember at times, we're not alone in our confusion. Learning the fullness of God's ability to define reality was a continuing lesson for the disciples. We see this repeatedly in the Gospels as they tried to find the lowest common denominator (the minimum amount of effort required) in following Jesus. For example, as Jesus was setting out on a journey, a man ran up and knelt before him, and asked him, "Teacher, what good deed must I do to have eternal life?" Jesus replied, "Why do you ask me about what is good? There is only one who is good. If you wish to enter into life, keep the commandments" (Matthew 19:16–17). Caught on low thresholds, as is the temptation of those seduced by comfortable lives, the rich young man wanted to have his cake and eat it too. He asked Jesus which commandments he needed to keep to have eternal life (Matthew 19:18). The question gave away his immaturity in the spiritual life because it showed that the young rich man wanted to do the minimum amount and still have great rewards. But Jesus tried to expand the definitions already established of what and who is good. "You shall not murder; You shall not commit adultery; You shall not steal; You shall not bear false witness; Honor your father and mother; also, You shall love your neighbor as yourself" (Matthew 19:18–19). The man responded, "I have kept all these; what do I still lack?" (Matthew 19:20). Using Mark's account of this same story, Jesus, "looking at [the young rich man], loved him and said, 'You lack one thing; go, sell what you own, and give the money to the poor, and you will have treasure in heaven; then come, follow me'" (Mark 10:21). It is interesting that Mark records that Jesus looked at the young rich man, and in looking at him loved him. In other words, Jesus had compassion on the man as a parent would have compassion on a child who was trying to understand grownup things but couldn't. Needless to say, when the man looked back at Jesus, he was shocked and went away grieving, because he had many toys from which he could not be separated.

The disciples were probably standing around watching this scene transpire, amused until what happened next. Then Jesus looked at them with the same parental look and said to his disciples, "How hard it will be for those who have wealth to enter the kingdom of God!" You wouldn't think this of the disciples, those we hold in such high esteem as apostles and saints, but they too were aiming for great power and wealth with low thresholds to cross. They even argued about who would be the greatest in heaven without taking into account the difficulties in getting there (Mark 10:35–40). Jesus' gaze toward them in Mark 10 perplexed the disciples. And notice again how Jesus responds as a parent, "Children, how hard it is to enter the kingdom of God! It is easier for a camel to go through the eye of a needle than for someone who is rich to enter the kingdom of God" (Mark 10:24–25). They were greatly astounded and said to one another, "Then who can be saved?" (Mark 10:26). If we imagine the disciples as saints, if we picture them all like male Mother Teresas, then why do they ask this question? Why do they make the issue of wealth the linchpin of existence?

The way we think about the disciples must be no different from the way we think about ourselves. The saving grace for the disciples was not any extraordinary spirituality given to them alone—no, they were just like us, only with the extreme gift of Jesus' physical presence. Finally, Jesus provides the "punch line" of the parable: "For mortals it is impossible, but not for God; *for God all things are possible*" (Mark 10:27, emphasis mine).

For God all things are possible. That's an understanding we need to inhabit deeply if we're going to be reconciling people. Too often we think we know how to define someone else, or that we know the only solution to a problem, or that we know what God can do or can't do. We keep forgetting that God can do even the impossible, and that God has already done the impossible and reconciled us. Our task is to live into that.

Does God Love Manuel Noriega?

It's easy to read the material above about recognizing God's infinite abilities and not be overly challenged by it. Let me ask you to think about it in terms that are more concrete by considering the story of Manuel Noriega.

At the end of the award-winning film, *Noriega: God's Favorite*, Bob Hoskins, playing Panamanian dictator Manuel Noriega, asks: "Why does God love Tony Noriega? Why does he forgive him? How did I get to be his favorite? Why does he give me this third act? Because, I think, he wants me to begin again. And this time, Father, I assure you I will not let you down."[3]

Just before surrendering his life in the movie (based on historical facts), Noriega begins a confession of his life story to a Catholic priest. Noriega takes refuge at Panama's Vatican embassy, residence of the papal ambassador. The movie begins with a radical priest (Father Jorge) describing how Noriega had a resistance leader, Dr. Hugo Spadafora, killed. In the film, Father Jorge states, "[Spadafora] was serially raped and they severed his hamstrings so he couldn't resist. Then they drove a stake up his ass."

The papal ambassador responds, "Before the drug money came there was never such torture and pain."

Father Jorge continues, "Unfortunately, the torture didn't kill him, he was still alive when they cut off his head."

The papal ambassador concludes, "The great Dr. Spadafora. You know this time the little general [referring to Noriega], if it is him, has gone too far."

The writers and director of the film expertly complicate the characters. For example, despite the righteous tone of the papal ambassador and the horrific description of Noriega's past by Father Jorge, in the rest of the movie, Noriega is an equal debater. Noriega states to the papal ambassador: "All those years in the Vatican you must have developed some sympathy for the point of view of the devil," implying that the Vatican itself was full of deceit and intrigue.

The papal ambassador awkwardly responds, "Well, [my experience in the Vatican] has given me . . . a certain moral range."

Later, near the end of the movie, when Noriega has taken refuge at the Vatican embassy, Father Jorge refuses to give communion to Noriega. After overtly passing over a kneeling Noriega with his outstretched hands, Father Jorge (the most anti-Noriega priest in Panama) later says to the papal ambassador: "[Noriega] has to make a confession. He has to have an act of contrition, otherwise he is committing another mortal sin by accepting communion."

The papal ambassador responds, "But it is his sin . . . Father . . . not yours. You are not the judge. You are only the priest."

Father Jorge responds, "Really, Monsignor, do you really think God loves this man?"

The papal ambassador concludes with a sigh, "Is it not obvious?"

This film's portrayal of Noriega illustrates the second problem of holding up negative examples: We are easily tempted to bring quickly to mind those to whom we could never be reconciled without recognizing that they could be moving away from evil practices. This film expertly demonstrates the problem. The very title, *Noriega: God's Favorite*, illustrates the anomaly of how God's ways are often not our ways.

The film opens with the words that Panama is a small, impoverished republic that connects the two Americas. But it contains a treasure of enormous value: the Panama Canal. Like his country, Gen. Manuel Antonio Noriega was born in poverty and grew up in neglect. Illegitimate and orphaned by his mother, he learned to survive in the slums of Panama City. He became a CIA informer while still in military school. Noriega seized power in 1983 after Gen. Omar Torrijos died in a plane crash. Soon after, civil wars and drug traffickers thrust his long-ignored country and its corrupt leader onto the world stage.

In March 1999, General Noriega's forty-year sentence for racketeering and drug trafficking was reduced. He was eligible for parole in 2000. Despite the tragic-comedic tone of Bob Hoskins' portrayal of Noriega, fourteen Americans and more than nineteen hundred Panamanians died during the U.S. invasion of Panama. Since Noriega's ouster, drug traffic through Panama has doubled. Noriega was convicted in absentia by a Panamanian court for his role in the murder of Spadafora and the coup ringleaders. He received three twenty-year prison terms. In April 1999, Panamanian authorities formally requested his extradition.

Most of us, I would imagine, are like Father Jorge. We really don't think God could love such a person. Until we believe God can and does, however, the following discussion on exemplars of reconciliation can lead either to vicarious forms of practices of reconciliation or to static concepts of who in fact can be reconciled.

CHAPTER 5
Remembering God

Reconciliation is the slow, arduous work of the Christian vocation of dying to pathological selfhood and emerging into a new and glorious communal self. This work of being Christlike is not a quick fix, as has been demonstrated over two millennia. The slow, arduous work often involves discomfort and dis-ease. As St. Paul reminds us, we are being made into a new creation. Paul writes, "From now on, therefore, we regard [remember] no one from a human point of view [or according to *sarx*, the flesh]" (2 Corinthians 5:16). C. S. Lewis illustrates Paul's spiritual coaching when he writes:

> It is a serious thing to live in a society of possible gods and goddesses, *to remember* that the dullest and most uninteresting person you can talk to may one day be a creature which, if you saw it now, you would be strongly tempted to worship, or else a horror and a corruption such as you now meet, if at all, only in a nightmare. All day long we are, in some degree, helping each other to one or other of these destinations. . . . There are no *ordinary* people. You have never talked to a mere mortal. Nations, cultures, arts,

civilizations—these are mortal, and their life is to ours as the life of a gnat. But it is immortals whom we joke with, work with, marry, snub, and exploit—immortal horrors or everlasting splendors.[1]

I discovered this for myself as a child. One day in class I was talking while we were supposed to be quiet. "Who was talking?" my teacher Mrs. Harris asked. It was simply a rhetorical question, the kind that all third-grade public school teachers ask, not expecting a response from anyone. For some reason, I had to respond, shocking both Mrs. Harris and myself out of the rhetorical framework of the question. I raised my hand and made my confession, thereby disrupting Mrs. Harris's normal teaching method. I had to confess that I was talking because I had made a decision for my eight-year-old self that if God exists, I would have to behave as if God exists, behave as if I was fully transparent to God. "I did it, Mrs. Harris," I confessed. And this confession turned out to lead toward my repentance—my behaving as if God exists.

At first this felt like an awful change, because no longer could I throw my candy wrapper on the ground when no one was watching. I also had to help elderly people across the street in the absence of being rewarded by others. It felt awful at first, because my worldview expanded from "me" to "I in relationship to others." My most important "other" became God, of whom I was incessantly aware. The initial paranoia of remembering that God was always watching me transformed me into a healthier version of myself—into a communal person. From my third-grade year, I was invited into the mature way of seeing that my transparency in God increased my capacity of becoming a person capable of mutuality. Little did I realize, however, that I would repeat and remember confessions similar to my third-grade admission of guilt over and over again.

Such perpetual remembering is how I see the practice of reconciliation. Each of us, as a spiritual practice, must learn to remember God. We must learn to act in a way that illustrates that we believe God exists.

Perhaps one of the most difficult aspects of reconciliation is that we don't truly believe it's possible. Do you remember the story in John's gospel of the royal official in Cana who came to Jesus hoping that Jesus would heal his ailing son? That's all he wanted from Jesus. But perhaps, even though he was asking for it, he didn't believe it would happen, because the first thing Jesus says to the official is: "Unless you see signs and wonders you will not believe" (4:48). Then Jesus simply says: "Go; your son will live" (4:50). Of course, the royal official returns home, not necessarily in faith, but in curiosity and expectation. He finally sees the miracle of the healing when he first arrives, but has to resort to his memory to have faith. John describes it this way: "As he was going down, his slaves met him and told him that his child was alive. So he asked them the hour when he began to recover, and they said to him, 'Yesterday at one in the afternoon the fever left him.' The father realized that this was the hour when Jesus had said to him, 'Your son will live.' So he himself believed, along with his whole household" (4:51–53). We honor the official for eventually having faith in this Johannine account, but we are haunted by the tone of Jesus' words: "Unless you see signs and wonders you will not believe." Why can't we just remember the power of God always, without the addictive need to see signs of power? I think the prophet Isaiah gives us the answer.

God speaks in Isaiah 65 about developing a new vision, about wiping the old slate clean and starting from scratch, "For I am about to create new heavens and a new earth; the former things shall not be remembered or come to mind" (v. 17). God promises us a new heaven and a new earth, but it is so difficult to actually believe in and trust those words. We have to continually remind ourselves of God's vision for us with hand gestures, with ink on paper, with bread and wine, and through the painful awareness of sin and our need for reconciliation. The new heaven and earth that God has planted in us is bold and reinvigorating, but it is challenging to hold on to. According to Isaiah's God, the psalmist is no longer right about our life span. No longer are we destined to live only seventy years (eighty if we're lucky). In Isaiah's vision, God says to us, "for one who dies at a hundred years will be considered a youth, and one who falls short of a hundred will be considered accursed" (v. 20). No longer will global practices of injustice exist. Kenyan farmers will no longer grow crops that they cannot use for their benefit, growing coffee beans for transnational companies that cheat them out of the market. No longer will brown people build cities that they cannot inhabit. God says, "They shall build houses and inhabit them; they shall plant vineyards and eat their fruit. They shall not build and another inhabit; they shall not plant and another eat" (vv. 21–22).

God will create new memories in us that will stick. We won't have to seek signs and wonders to believe God exists because we will become the living memory of God. As embodied memories, we require an expressive spirituality if memory is to be retained at all. By inhabiting God's new ways, we can solve the problem of memory—that is, we constantly forget that which needs to be reconciled and move on to the next conflict without sufficient memory of how we may have failed to reconcile the last conflict. Like a pack of dogs in a fight, we forget who we are kin to and easily turn on each other. Through Isaiah's witness, we learn to embody the memory of God instead of our own mistaken images of the world God has created. The fable of the Lion and the Rabbit recounted below illustrates this very human tendency.

While he was growing up in rural South Africa, Tinyiko Sam Maluleke's grandmother and aunts delighted in telling him fables of Rabbit and Lion as they sat around the fire in the open-air makeshift "kitchen" called *xivava*. The fables consisted of various living characters drawn from humanity, animals, and nature in general, but Lion and Rabbit fables always occupied a special place. The point of them appeared to be simple: although Lion was big, strong and powerful, he was not smart enough to match wits with Rabbit. Even the apparently weak and vulnerable, like Rabbit, have creative resources for changing conflict situations into flourishing states. These fables were recounted in animated and highly entertaining ways that always succeeded in providing moral formation for children growing up. One particular Lion and Rabbit fable—told in a variety of versions—has been extremely popular.

Lion has been traversing the length and breadth of the land searching for Rabbit. In a series of clever antics and tricks, Rabbit has made a fool of Lion again and again. This has stripped Lion of every shred of dignity and respect among his fellow animals, and Lion has become a pitiable laughing stock. Fuming with anger and frustration, Lion is now going for the "final solution." He's going to get rid of Rabbit once and for all. After a whole day's search, Lion's efforts bear fruit. Quite by chance, as Lion walks home he finds Rabbit feasting on a meal so scrumptious that he does not even notice Lion standing at the mouth of the cave.

> "Aha! Got you! Today is the day when you die, little friend," he growls as he carefully and slowly enters the cave so that Rabbit has no escape route.
>
> In a typical flash of inspiration, Rabbit shouts: "Lion, please be careful, the cave is about to collapse and kill us both. You are the strong one, please hold up the roof of the cave while I go and seek help." Caught in the urgency of the situation, Lion springs onto his hind legs and holds up the roof with his front legs as Rabbit dashes out of the cave—never to return.

Most of us in the Western world think we have already figured out the moral of this story—that we should learn to be clever like the rabbit in matters of survival. But Maluleke, our African sage, teaches us Western children to go further and ask: Is Rabbit that noble a character after all? Is there nothing to be said for Lion's generosity in suspending a selfish desire for revenge in the light of what he believed to be a much more serious calamity? Is there no grace in cooperating with one's mortal enemy in times of crisis? What if the roof had indeed been collapsing? Would we not sing the praises of Lion, the unselfish one? Then Rabbit would have been exposed as selfish and small-minded. Lion holds the roof when Rabbit flies giggling away, enjoying the good life in some other corner of the world. That is to say, the moral of the story is not without complexity. "The stupidity of Lion is not without its redeeming qualities, nor is the inventive intelligence of rabbit without its flaws."[2]

Like our African sage Maluleke, God will plant a vision in us of how to inhabit new heavens and a new earth. We will have to use our lateral thinking or our wisdom, however, to learn the lessons so that God's lessons will stick with us and create new realities. Classical theology tends to make reconciliation something innate to God, reaching us as a finished product. Our violent existence rejects such speculation, however. One of the most astounding realities is that although churches are home to both lions and rabbits, facilitating reconciliation has not come naturally to them. "As we look at ourselves and at our hungry, poor, abused, and war-torn world, do we weep? Are we appalled at the evil around us and at the evil lodged securely in our own hearts?"[3] Reconciliation is a something that needs to be made and "orchestrated."[4]

Herein is the great problem of being a Christian in what is now known as post-Christendom. It is that the episodic life of the memory of being Christian often slips away without any chance of encapsulation. As Maggie Ross in her book *Pillars of Flame* believes, many Western Christians no longer remember their baptisms and therefore need to be ordained out of this insecurity.[5] We struggle with the meaning of being Christian today without the skills and habits of living into the identity that represents God's reconciliation of the world. Dom Helder Camara explains, "Let no one be scandalized if I frequent those who are considered unworthy or sinful. Who is not a sinner? Let no one be alarmed if I am seen with compromised and dangerous people, on the left or the right. Let no one bind me to a group. My door, my heart, must be open to everyone, absolutely everyone."[6] It is from such an embodied Christian as Camara that one may begin to imagine the embodiment of reconciliation.

Coaching from Paul

What I understand as reconciliation comes from St. Paul's exhortation to the community of Corinth: "[God] has given us the ministry of reconciliation" (2 Corinthians 5:18). Reconciliation (*katallage*) means the restoration of relationship gone awry between God and humanity through repentance and trust in the expiatory death of Christ. My focus here is on the ongoing problem of relationships gone awry and how we may live more deeply into the meaning of *katallage*.[7]

We learn from Paul that the Christian's need is to live into practices of reconciliation and repentance like an athlete trains to reach a goal. The world of Paul and our world hold many similarities. Back then and still now, we look at our troubled church and world and fear for our lives. But the writer of the letter to the Ephesians sought to encourage a fainthearted community through the theological worldview that God destines us for grace and peace in Christ. Ultimately, such grace and peace become markers toward the goal of unity in God.

If I gave you a short length of ribbon or yarn, what would you do? Chances are you could think of something to make with your individual piece of string. Another approach, however, is that we could all join our short pieces of yarn together and make a longer rope. And many more uses could be found for the long rope than for the many short pieces of rope. The same is true of individuals and what happens when they join in unity to be "church." But, as in Paul's time, we lack such unity—sometimes even the vision of it. In Paul's day, most people explained troubling events as the capriciousness of numerous gods and goddesses who lived above the world but cared little about the fate of human beings. In contrast, Paul trusted the one true, loving God in Jesus Christ who wants us to live with God. Our role is to make visible the destiny of our unity in Christ, but what gets in the way of our display of this destiny? Who supports us in finishing the race we began in baptism?

Paul begs a community to practice being in Christ by forgiving each other's offenses and by practicing repentance instead of constantly living into the violent, undisciplined, negative Corinthian stereotypes. Paul writes, "But if anyone has caused pain, he has caused it not to me, but to some extent—not to exaggerate it—to all of you" (2 Corinthians 2:5). For Paul, the urgency involved is in remembering and recalling the mystery of the *imago Dei* in us to be more than *sarx* or flesh—animals that live simply according to instinctual urge.

As Paul found it a complex task to ask the Corinthian community to practice forgiveness and reconciliation, I would imagine it is difficult for Western churches typecast by recent developments of compartmentalized conservative/liberal typologies to know how to be true communities. After all, it is difficult to ask Western Christians to practice reconciliation and repentance if all that really needs to be forgiven is a self, not whole communities. It would be much easier to think about forgiveness and reconciliation if such concepts were self-defined. In other words, we each would have in mind what we personally want justified and reconciled. The problem, however, is that this leads to relativism, in which it becomes hard to tell how to rectify your needs over my needs. If reconciliation is to take place, we must become communal persons, people capable of integrating the personal and the communal. Stanley Hauerwas's prayer helps me illustrate this point. Hauerwas wrote the prayer for a vigil against the death penalty held on April 16, 2002. The vigil was organized by a student of my Spiritualty of Nonviolence class, Michael Barham.

> For God's sake, God, why cannot you grant us vengeance? Can you feel the pain, the terror, the horror, of murder? Can you not recognize the emptiness left in those left in the wake of murder? We want, we desperately desire, to have our world rid of those who kill without regret. We join our voice with the Psalmist for vengeance, for the recovery of our world. Eye for an eye.
>
> But it is not "our" world. It is your world. Vengeance, it turns out, is yours not ours. It seems, moreover, you will not trust us with your vengeance. After all it was vengeance that killed your son. A killing that forever ended our attempts to make our world safe by killing. A hard lesson not easily learned. So we continue to kill in the name of vengeance, in the name of safety.

Make us, your church, desire not safety but the justice of your Son's cross. May we be for the world the embodiment of the justice shaped by charity found continually present in the Eucharist—the end of all sacrifice. Through that sacrifice make us a people who would rather die than kill. So made may we be the end of capital punishment.[8]

As I stated in the introduction to this book, the current tensions between the right and left, the rich and poor, those of color and those called white, women and men, homosexual and heterosexual—these are tensions today, but our solutions cannot simply come from a consensus of individual ideas, because such a consensus will never occur, but from spiritual practices focused on making the personal and the communal interdependent. E. J. Dionne helps me explain:

Many are looking for a path that allows us to begin reconciling the concerns of those, mostly on the right, who see our country's troubles as primarily moral in nature and those on the left, who speak of our problems in terms of economic and social injustice. The two are inextricably linked. You cannot have family values without social justice, and you cannot have social justice without strong and loving families. You cannot reduce poverty without reducing crime, and you cannot reduce crime without expanding opportunity for the poor. If you worry about a culture of violence, you may have to talk to both Hollywood and the NRA. If you want to eradicate racism, you have to expand the economic opportunities of people of all races. If you worry about sexism, you have to see men and women as both parents and producers. If you want government to work, you have to worry about those institutions outside government, the institutions of civil society, that give people realistic hope that action in common produces results worth working for.[9]

Christians should know that a consensus of ideas never comes without practice. This is what Paul tried to get the early church to understand. For Paul, to live according to the flesh simply means to follow the instinctual urge toward destruction of self and community. Such an instinctual self is what I think Jesus has in mind when he instructs us to live into the paradox of losing our life to find it (Matthew 10:39). "So if anyone is in Christ, there is a new creation: everything old has passed away; see, everything has become new! All this is from God, who reconciled us to himself through Christ, and has given us the ministry of reconciliation" (2 Corinthians 5:17–18).

The paradox in all of this is that Paul is coaching the Corinthian community to remember that all things have passed away, in other words, to do the paradoxical work of remembering that they live in a new reality. This remembering of a new reality is really what we mean as repentance; like an injured athlete trains over and over to make his human body remember new and correct movements, repentance is the Christian's training over and over to remember new life. Earlier, I tried to illustrate this remembering of new reality through my epiphany when I was in third grade at Sherwood Bates Elementary School in Raleigh, North Carolina. I had to confess that I was talking in class because I made a decision for my eight-year-old self that, if God exists, *I would have to behave as if God exists*, behave like I believed that my life was fully transparent to God. "I did it, Mrs. Harris," I confessed. And this confession turned out to lead toward my repentance—my behaving as if God exists.

Little did I realize, however, that my third-grade confession would have to be repeated and remembered over and over again. Such perpetual remembering is how I see the practice of reconciliation. It is impossible for us as human beings to retain anything as a pure memory; instead, we must embody memory. And the way that Paul teaches not only Christians of his time but us as well is through this conclusion: "All this is from God, who reconciled us to himself through Christ, and has given us the ministry of reconciliation" (2 Corinthians 5:18). Paul helps us see that God has already done the ultimate work for us. Our task becomes the embodiment of Christ's memory practiced through the ministry of reconciliation.

CHAPTER 6
Practicing God's Ways

Reconciliation, as a concept, assumes people are always in need of it. In other words, we can easily fall into mistakes without knowing it, and before long we end up living in these mistakes as if they were our normality. A fish, for example, doesn't know that it's wet. Until our view of what is normal encounters a reference point (as when a fish finds itself on the floor of a boat), we can easily think our mistakes are really our perfections. This is the ultimate problem of reconciliation.

How do we know what needs to be reconciled in our lives and what such reconciliation looks like? In short, it's difficult to define reconciliation. Defining reconciliation is the same problem encountered by Peter, who thought he understood rational definitions (e.g., the definition of forgiveness, Matthew 18:21–22). Jesus, however, broke open Peter's definition to push him deeper into the process of defining reconciliation—moving him toward learning how to define the ineffable. For example, Peter was not just to forgive completely, as the number seven suggests, but he was called to forgive beyond calculation—seventy times seven (Matthew 18:21–22). Peter's mistakes are our mistakes. And thank God for Peter, because we are called to learn from such mistakes and not repeat them.

The mistake we make in trying to understand God's work of reconciliation is based on our need to control the nature and scope of God's accomplishment. Our own need to understand the parameters of divine reconciliation often leads to vapid understandings of reconciliation. At best, the need to define the divine work of reconciliation leads to static concepts of heaven and hell that inform similar mutually exclusive earthly realities. If we really believed in a God who creates *ex nihilo*, we would practice restorative justice more often, realizing, like the psalmist, that even in hell God seeks our salvation. But our understandings of reconciliation are too often informed by self-interest instead of by God's mercy. Do we forgive simply out of self-interest? Because we love humanity? Or because we want to imitate God? There is probably a bit of all three in most decisions to forgive, but not always. Ultimately, reconciliation depends on whether I am forgiving to get rid of an ulcer or because I find myself in love with humanity and with God.

How do we practice reconciliation when those who need to be reconciled keep changing, like ships passing in the night, and when self-interested individuals are incapable of seeing communal connections? Instead of settling upon static definitions of reconciliation, I propose that our Christian tradition urges us toward inhabiting the spiritual practices of reconciliation. We must learn to inhabit practices of reconciliation that lead toward living more faithfully into God's mission of reconciliation, so that when past, present, and future conflicts arise, we are equipped to negotiate such conflicts openly and even to discover resolution. We need to learn how to inhabit or practice reconciliation in a way that makes us vulnerable and transparent to each other as we seek to respond to God's call to live into the divine work of reconciliation already accomplished but not yet fully realized. To practice reconciliation is to develop the habit of seeing beyond the natural instinct of retaliation.

An important habit necessary for overcoming the tendency to limit God's definition of reconciliation is to resist stereotypes. Every age has had its mean-spirited epithets for people considered the "other," and today is no exception. The so-called War on Terrorism has spawned a whole new generation of them. During

World War II, Americans became "Amis" to the Germans. To Americans, Germans were "Krauts." Vietnam had its "gooks," and now, the War on Terrorism has its own dehumanizing name: "hajji." That's what many U.S. troops across Iraq and in coalition bases in Kuwait now call anyone from the Middle East or South Asia. Soldiers who served in Afghanistan say it is also used there.

Among Muslims, the word is used mainly as a title of respect. It means "one who has made the hajj," the pilgrimage to Mecca. That's not how Western soldiers use it. Some talk about "killing some hajjis" or "mowing down some hajjis." One soldier in Iraq inked "Hodgie Killer" onto his footlocker. Iraqis, friend or foe, are called hajjis. Kuwaitis are called hajjis. Even people brought in by civilian contractors to work in mess halls or drive buses are hajjis— despite the fact that they might be from India, the Philippines, or Pakistan, and might be Hindu or Christian. The souvenir stands found on even the smallest U.S. bases in the Middle East and run by locals are called hajji shops. A cluster of small businesses inside a larger base is " Hajji Town." The word has become the most obvious evidence of the deep gulf between the traditional cultures of the Middle East and Afghanistan and the young men and women of the U.S. military. Soldiers often have little knowledge of local culture beyond a ninety-minute briefing they get before deployment. An unnamed spokesman for U.S. Central Command in Baghdad said that the term was troubling but that there had been no official order to stop its use. "This is more of a common sense thing," he said. "It's like using any other derogatory word for a racial or ethnic group. Some may use it in a joking way, but it's derogatory, and I'm sure people have tried to stop it."

In Iraq, there is little interaction between U.S. soldiers and the people they came to liberate. Soldiers in the most dangerous parts of Iraq, such as the Sunni Triangle west and north of Baghdad, seldom have contact with Iraqis except to train guns on them from passing Humvees as they scan for weapons. Their officers say the situation makes it easy to view all Iraqis as a faceless, dangerous mass, even though many civilians are friendly, so they try hard to humanize Iraqis to reduce the likelihood of wrongful shootings.

"Hajji," one person said, sounds like the racist terms that U.S. soldiers used in the 1991 Persian Gulf War, such as "towel-head." The term brings back disturbing memories for those who spent time in Vietnam during that war. "That sounds familiar," said John Balaban, a North Carolina State University English professor and poet-in-residence who has written about Vietnam and the war. As a conscientious objector, Balaban did alternative service in Vietnam. "There were several words—'Gook,' 'Slope,' 'Dink,'" he said. "Some of these were meaningless, but they were all working toward the same goal, of trivializing and depersonalizing the enemy. It makes it easier to kill these people and not feel bad about it."[1]

But is that a good thing, that we can easily kill someone else and not feel bad about it? How does that affect our understandings of reconciliation?

Why Reconciliation?

Now this bell tolling softly for another says to me, you must die. No one is an island, entire of itself; everyone is a piece of the continent, a part of the main . . . Anyone's death diminishes me because I am involved in humankind, and therefore never send to know for whom the bell tolls; it tolls for you.[2]

Christian faith was born in a conflicted world. Isn't it tempting to just resign ourselves to the idea that conflict is all there is and just get on with life? In this book, however, I want to challenge you with a different question: Why reconciliation? Richard Mouw again helps me explain, using the contentious issues of sexual orientation in the church:

> This is an important time for each of us to be honest about our sexual condition. We evangelicals have nothing to brag about in this area. It is not enough for us to tell those with whom we disagree strongly about sexual orientation questions how wrong we think they are. Nor is it very helpful for other folks to keep insisting that we can solve most of our theological problems in this area by focusing

on a Jesus who cares deeply about a generic, unnuanced "inclusivity." If that is all we have to say to each other, there is no hope for the continuing unity of our denomination.[3]

Mouw's insight moves us away from the natural acceptance of perpetual conflict and into the pursuit of connecting worldviews that appear incommensurate. But this takes perpetual practice. The answer to why we need reconciliation goes deeper than our own self-interests, deeper even than what we individually settle upon as justice. We need reconciliation, because without it we are unable to see God's intended reconciliation. To practice the presence of God requires the practice of reconciliation—whether we want to be reconciled or not. Herein was Jesus' earthly work: to show us this truth.

Jesus' fame had spread, according to Matthew (5:43-45), so much so that even though Jesus resided mostly in the Galilee region, deeply conflicted people were flocking to him from what is now known as Syria, Lebanon, Jordan, Jerusalem, Israel/Palestine, and even from what is now Iraq. The people who came to him were all victims of war, disease, politics, and religion. They heard a different message from Jesus than the standard "survival of the fittest" themes. Jesus gave them a new way of seeing: "You have heard that it was said, 'You shall love your neighbor and hate your enemy.' But I say to you, Love your enemies and pray for those who persecute you" (Matthew 5:43-44).

Jesus knew the right lesson to teach, a lesson that continues to be difficult for us to learn. Jesus continues: "[I]f you love those who love you, what reward do you have?" (Matthew 5:46). Maybe this wasn't as rhetorical a question as we might imagine, because Jesus was preaching to people who came to learn ultimate solutions. Maybe some in the crowd answered his question, "What reward do you have?" by answering in the following manner: "Well, if we love ourselves, we could maintain own culture." Others may have said, "If we love those who love us, we could maintain the purity of our own heritage." Still others may have said, "If we love those who it is natural for us to love, at least we could continue to speak our native tongue, Aramaic, instead of having it wiped out by oppressive cultures." "If we follow this strange teaching of loving our enemies," they concluded, "then we lose to our enemies and oppressors, the Roman Empire." I would imagine Jesus listened to them as the sun began to set.

Jesus' response was not hotheaded, idealistic, or apolitical. He heard their deep need. He responded: "Do not even the tax collectors [one of the most despised persons of Jesus' days] do the same?" Matthew, himself a tax collector, recording these events, especially wants us to hear this teaching of Jesus. Jesus continues, "If you greet only your brothers and sisters, what more are you doing than others" to show forth the fullness of the kingdom of heaven? (Matthew 5:46–47). Jesus then makes a very interesting parallel between *loving* your enemies and *praying* for those who persecute you and *being* children. To love our enemies does not involve putting flowers in your hair and listening to Bob Dylan. Loving your enemies isn't about weakness. To love our enemies is not some axiom only to be appreciated for its aesthetic value but disregarded in the real world. No, Jesus says that to love our enemies requires three actions. In Matthew 5:43–45, Jesus makes parallel the verbs *to love* (first), then *to pray* (second), and then *to be* children.

The point of Jesus' preaching to the people of Syria, Lebanon, Jordan, Iraq, to Jerusalem, Israel/Palestine, the United States, the United Kingdom—the meaning for all of us is: *If you want to know that you are more than violent animals, you will have to behave as if prayer is more than talking to yourself—to pray is to love.* Jesus' lesson for the first century, for our century, and for future centuries is that diverse peoples must learn to desire to pass beyond their individual understandings of reality and reorient themselves in the ways of God, who allows the sun to rise on the evil and the good; who sends the rain on the righteous and on the unrighteous. Jesus is teaching us a hard lesson: If we can love the other, those of other cultures, other nations, even other worldviews, we will open ourselves to the higher reality that we are all children of God.

Why reconciliation? The answer is simple: Because it makes us God's children—related to God. We are related to God when we learn to live in higher realities than violence and death. When Jesus said, "Be perfect . . . as your heavenly Father is perfect" (Matthew 5:48), it means that our humanity lies in the perfection of children who are discovering their identities through relationships. So, Jesus tells us to pray not with words, but by working through difficult relationships, like those with our enemies (Matthew 5:6–15). To learn to see an enemy as our sister or brother is the truest form of prayer, because we are being made into children of God. "As a father has compassion for his children, so the Lord has compassion for those who fear him" (Psalm 103:13). We become children of God when the reality of death cannot define us Our prayer becomes: "Deliver us, O Lord, from our impregnable, invulnerable selves, for in our safety, we learn to doubt your true power."

If we aren't careful, we may create God in our own image, and therefore only talk to ourselves and call it prayer. Little Leroy helps me explain:

> Little Leroy came into the kitchen where his mother was making dinner. His birthday was coming up and he thought this was a good time to tell his mother what he wanted. "Mom, I want a bike for my birthday." Little Leroy was a bit of a troublemaker. He had gotten into trouble at school and at home. Leroy's mother asked him if he thought he deserved to get a bike for his birthday. Little Leroy, of course, thought he did. Leroy's mother, being a Christian woman, wanted him to reflect on his behavior over the last year and write a letter to God and tell him why he deserved a bike for his birthday. Little Leroy stomped up the steps to his room and sat down to write God a letter.

Letter 1

> Dear God,
> I have been a very good boy this year and I would like a bike for my birthday. I want a red one.
> Your friend,
> Leroy

Leroy knew this wasn't true. He had not been a very good boy, so he tore up the letter and started over.

Letter 2

Dear God,
This is your friend Leroy. I have been a pretty good boy this year, and I would like a red bike for my birthday.
Thank you,
Leroy

Leroy knew this wasn't true either. He tore up the letter and started again.

Letter 3

Dear God,
I have been an okay boy this year and I would really like a red bike for my birthday.
Leroy

Leroy knew he could not send this letter to God either, so he wrote another letter.

Letter 4

Dear God,
I know I haven't been a good boy this year. I am very sorry. I will be a good boy if you just send me a red bike for my birthday. Thank you,
Leroy

Leroy knew, even if it was true, this letter was not going to get him a bike. By now, Leroy was very upset. He went downstairs and told his mother he wanted to go to church. Leroy's mother thought her plan had worked because Leroy looked very sad. "Just be home in time for dinner," his mother said.

Leroy walked down the street to the church and up to the altar. He looked around to see if anyone was there. He picked up a statue of the Virgin Mary. He slipped it under his shirt and ran out of the church, down the street, into his house, and up to his room. He shut the door to his room and sat down with a piece of paper and a pen. Leroy began to write his letter to God.

Letter 5

> I've got your mama. If you want to see her again, send the bike.
> Signed,
> You know who

Sadly, we are Little Leroy. We still pray like him. Prayer, ultimately, is the means of relationship in which we recognize the living God. No one can pray without such relationship. This was the Pharisee's problem in Jesus' parable. He thought he could pray to God without being related to the tax collector. "God, I thank you that I am not like other people: thieves, rogues, adulterers, or even like this tax collector" (Luke 18:11). The mistake of Leroy and the Pharisee is that they thought they were capable of prayer on their own, but the mystery of prayer is that we cannot know God without knowing our neighbor and—an even more difficult requirement—without loving our enemies. Developing the character to know our neighbor and to love our enemies requires our discerning the presence of God among outcasts and the rejected of the world. We do this because Christians are not called simply to love the lovable, but to be reconciled with all people.

Too often, we look at others and compare ourselves to them. And often, we come up short. We look and say, "Oh she's twenty-five and she's done this, this, this, and this." Or we watch people who "have it all together" and we begin to put ourselves down. We find any number of ways to compare ourselves to others—and come up short. But the grass is always greener on the other side. Stop comparing yourself to others. Each of us has his or her own thorns. Be it weight, single parenting, job dissatisfaction, husband problems, financial distress, children woes, overworked/underpaid issues, loneliness, confusion, self-doubt, etc. You've got to learn to love as Christ loves, and if you can't do that right now, at least quit comparing yourself to others, because you don't know what they are going through. Someone will always be prettier or more handsome than you. Someone will always be smarter than you. Someone's house will be bigger than yours. Someone will drive a better car. Someone's children will do better in school. And someone's husband will fix more things around the house than yours. So let it go, and invite a new kind of love in your life.

Prayer as relationship, rather than as words, challenges the impotent meanings of prayer, those false prayers that we want to keep praying. When faced with the complicated prospect of relating to others, many people say "I'll pray about it" to avoid a practical response or the strain of relatedness. But prayer isn't about avoiding the messiness of life. If we avoid the messiness, the church loses its identity.

The church finds itself in an identity crisis when its members do not practice the messiness of reconciliation on a regular basis. In fact, one may argue that until Christians understand reconciliation as our primary work in the world, we will never understand Christian identity. Because of colonialism and a multitude of wrongs done in the name of Christianity, inhabiting practices of reconciliation becomes vital to understanding who we are and why we are. A question-and-answer session with former Bishop John Shelby Spong helps me explain the confusion of wrongs done in the name of Christianity. A writer asked Bishop Spong, "Since you say that any god who can be killed should be killed, is it not fair to say that if Christianity can die, or should die, it must die?" Spong replied with a simple "Yes." He answered that if Christianity can die, then it should die. "If Christianity needs you or me to defend it from real or imagined enemies, it is surely in bad shape."

The real question for Spong is: What is Christianity? "Is it what the Pope says it is? Is it what Billy Graham says it is? Is it what Al Sharpton says it is? Or Jerry Falwell or James Kennedy or Robert Schuler?" Spong feels that various defenders of Christianity discover that when each defines what he or she believes Christianity to be, there is no consensus. This is so because of the changing face of Christianity throughout history. There was a time when the Pope was married, when the church taught that to invest money for interest was a sin, when slavery was allowed, and when critical thinkers were burned at the stake. Spong concludes,

> All of this leads me to assert that Christianity is not a fixed system that was born at the first Pentecost and might die in the twenty-first century. Christianity is a way people journey into the mystery of God. It is a process not unlike the ocean, it never changes its substance but it ever changes its form. People who want to defend or protect Christianity have always defined it in such a way as to make an idol out of their definition. An idol always dies. A channel through which the living God is ever revealed never does. Christianity may be transformed but it will not die. . . . So enter the stream of history that has been called Christianity and allow it to carry you in ways you cannot imagine into the mystery of God.[4]

Some have even argued that the church's missions must focus on "moving toward mutual relationship in Jesus Christ across and through significant differences." Willis Jenkins is helpful here, as he believes that Christian mission is the practice of rendering the self susceptible to the Holy Spirit, who in turn shows us the presence of Christ in the work and persons of those different from ourselves.[5] In the same vein, Archbishop William Temple (1881–1944) said that the church is the only society in the world that exists for the sake of those who are not its members. If we are to truly understand and inhabit reconciliation, we need to recognize that it is not abstract but concrete, involving real individuals and communities.

One practical suggestion that Jenkins makes is the practice of pilgrimage; that is, sending and hosting as a formational discipline for our church as a way of being with others and most importantly as a mode of inhabiting reconciliation. In other words, Christians are to practice pilgrimage in a way that we are sent forth into diverse places (e.g., geographical, socioeconomic, ethnic). And we are to host the same. Kerry Walters helps us see why the practice of pilgrimage (through the context of hosting) is so important in his recent book, *Jacob's Hip*. He begins his book this way: "This little book might never have been written but for the grandmotherly woman who walked out of church one morning and gave me the finger."[6]

Kerry Walters was leading a campaign for nonviolent resistance outside of his church immediately following the tragedy of September 11, 2001. His fellow Christians turned on him for engaging in nonviolent resistance. He continues to explain the messy response of those leaving church on Sunday morning, those who used words to call themselves Christians. Walters writes, "One older man driving past us actually pulled his well-groomed SUV to a brake-squealing halt, the better to bellow out: "You goddamn assholes! I just got through praying for pricks like you!""[7] If we are all children of God, we are all related; we don't get to choose our relatives. Being related to God often means having such family reunions. Being related to God reminds us that words are the least form of prayer. John reminds us in his epistle, "Those who say, 'I love God,' and hate their brothers or sisters, are liars; for those who do not love a brother or sister whom they have seen, cannot love God whom they have not seen" (1 John 4:20). Being related to God through Christ places us smack in the middle of a messy world in which we cannot love God without loving God through our ordinary and difficult relationships.

The good news for us is that Jesus reminds us not to grow weary, but simply to wade into deeper relationships, to slowly see God through the prayer of relating to others in this world in order to love God. Jesus says, "The greatest among you will be your servant" (Matthew 23:11). He doesn't just say this as some trite proverb to put into a hymnal. No, he commands his disciples to recognize this different kind of greatness so that they can recognize him (God incarnate) . . . so that they will recognize Jesus. Jesus' command anticipates the inability of his disciples to recognize him on the road to Emmaus after the crucifixion. If they had not been prepared to recognize the resurrected Jesus, their normal longing for a superman or military leader would have completely collapsed their vision. So, Jesus commands his disciples, "All who exalt themselves will be humbled, and all who humble themselves will be exalted" (Matthew 23:12). Again, he teaches this to the disciples to warn them, to teach them to recognize the risen Christ. Those going around this life thinking that greatness entails fame, who do everything so that people will see them in public, will have a hard time recognizing Jesus.

And if we are focused on recognizing Jesus, we are enabled to become enough of a person for God to be in relationship with. This view, of becoming enough of a person for God to commune with, safeguards our anthropomorphic tendencies of turning an abstracted humanity into God. Becoming enough of a person does not mean belittling your self esteem or trying to earn God's love. No, becoming a person means practicing the reality of God who in turn reflects our truer selves back to us—our *imago Dei*. It is in our humility that God needs to find our lost souls, our lost relationships, and reorient us so that prayer is achieved and God is seen through relatedness. We heed John's words that those who say they love God but hate others are liars. We must take heed; otherwise, we may confuse the lie with the truth. Kerry Walters explains:

> I believe that the disproportionately intense rage of my church lady points to a longstanding spiritual wound that all of us share, a wound whose carefully suppressed pain was traumatically aroused on 9/11. The resurfacing of this old ache is the root cause of the rage. The wound I'm referring to is the primordial and utterly threatening suspicion that life is unfixably unpredictable and unstable, that each individual must wage continuous battle against deadly dangers, and that each of us loses in the end anyway. . . .

> [W]e Christians have assumed we should be unafraid
> because we are under Christ's protection and thus insu-
> lated from worldly dangers. But this is false. . . . When
> we're told not to be afraid, the implication isn't that God's
> patronage somehow makes us invulnerable (the roll call
> of martyrs tells us this much), but rather that vulnerabil-
> ity isn't anything that ought to panic us.[8]

God's true power is relatedness. In such relatedness of triune persons, we discover our image of God as community. The *imago Dei*
is community. Martin Luther King Jr. helps us see the image of God
among us: "In a sense all life is interrelated. All men and women
are caught in an inescapable network of mutuality, tied in a single
garment of destiny. Whatever affects one directly affects all indi-
rectly. I can never be what I ought to be until you are what you
ought to be, and you can never be what you ought to be until I am
what I ought to be. This is the interrelated structure of reality."[9]

Strangely enough, our attention to God makes us also see ourselves through a vulnerable network of relationships. How can we
love God whom we do not see and hate our neighbor whom we
do see? The search of the human soul for meaning is really the
effort of staying in a committed relationship. Prayer is more like
living in a way in which my relationship with you gives me a language for God. A parishioner sent me the following story about the
power of relationship:

> A member of a certain church, who previously had been
> attending services regularly, suddenly stopped coming to
> church. After a few weeks, the priest decided to visit.
>
> The priest found the man at home alone, sitting before
> a blazing fire. Guessing the reason for his priest's visit, the
> man welcomed her, led her to a comfortable chair near the
> fireplace, and waited. The priest made herself at home but
> said nothing. In the grave silence, she contemplated the
> dance of the flames around the burning logs.

After some minutes, the priest took the fire tongs, carefully picked up a brightly burning ember, and placed it to one side of the hearth all alone.

Then she sat back in her chair, still silent. The host watched all this in quiet contemplation.

As the one lone ember's flame flickered and diminished, there was a momentary glow and then its fire was no more. Soon it was cold and lifeless.

The priest glanced at her watch and realized it was time to leave. She slowly stood up, picked up the cold, dead ember, and placed it back in the middle of the fire. Immediately it began to glow once more with the light and warmth of the burning coals around it.

As the priest reached the door to leave, her host said, with a tear running down his cheek, "Thank you so much for your visit and especially for the fiery sermon. I shall be back in church next Sunday."

Sometimes the best sermons are the ones left unspoken. Most of the time, just like the best sermons, the best prayers are those without words, those that happen through relationships. We live in a world that tries to say too much with too little. Consequently, few listen. Jesus knew that this was our predicament and taught the disciples to let their actions reflect their own meaning. Jesus said, "Let your light shine before others, so that they may see your good works and give glory to your Father in heaven" (Matthew 5:16). Jesus teaches—no, he commands his disciples—to use more than words to know God, to show reconciliation. Or as Yoda the wise sage says in *The Empire Strikes Back*: "Try not. Do, or do not. There is no try."

CHAPTER 7
Reconciliation as God's Apocalypse

One of the keys to religious experience is the shattering realization that no matter how hateful we are to ourselves, we are not hateful to God. This realization helps us to understand the difference between our love and His. Our love is a need. His love is a gift.

—Thomas Merton

Why is apocalyptic discourse important to the discussion of reconciliation? Author Alice Walker provides an answer. For example, Walker describes the refusal to forgive racism as "a stone; a knot in my psychic system."[1] In other words, there are some situations so severe that there isn't sufficient time and space to handle them in this life. The apocalypse or "the time after time ends" is important for reconciliation, because some accounts of reconciliation will have to wait for eternity—or at least until there is readiness and genuine repentance from the sinner.

Reconciliation is a process that involves not only practical action but also imagination. It dares us to imagine a better future, one that is based on the blessed possibility that injury will not be the final word that forecloses the future. It allows us to believe and trust that something new can happen. It is a sign that we have thrown in our lot with the Spirit's power to renew the face of the earth by breaking the destructive cycle of injury and revenge.

Three weeks into his first stint as pastor of an Indiana Bible Belt church, the Reverend Phillip Gulley, best-selling author of Christian stories set in fictional Harmony, Indiana, got a pink slip. "To get fired from a church somehow has the connotation that not only does the church not like you, but neither does God," Gulley said. Fuming church elders didn't find it funny that Gulley espoused the doctrine of universal salvation, which says all people, be they Muslims, Jews, Buddhists, Christians, or none of the above, are saved by God's grace. When Gulley refused to back off, they fired him. Now, years later, Gulley and his close friend, the Reverend James Mulholland, have co-written a book, *If Grace Is True: Why God Will Save Every Person*, which is drawing unabashed praise and stern criticism from concerned people of faith.[2]

In the apocalyptic visions of many people, there are two theologies. The first is retributive theology, in which few are saved based on a ransom theory of atonement explaining God's justice. Once a Christian invites Jesus into his or her heart, (thereby placating Jesus' vindictive Father), many Christians believe that he or she will go to heaven after death. The problem with this view of God's justice is in its definition of retribution (compensation for evil done, or vengeance) or restoration (bringing back to health or dignity, which is John's apocalyptic vision in Revelation 22:2). If justice is about retribution, then whose justice on earth is the best justice to use in identifying who goes to hell? The problem in answering the question is that one person's terrorist is another person's freedom fighter.

More acceptable to me is restorative theology, which says that creation is in much travail, and, because of this, God's relentless love will restore what is broken. In *Letters to a Young Poet*, the German poet Rainer Maria Rilke offers a profound definition of love: "Love is this—that two solitudes border, protect, and salute one another." Rilke avoids the invasive and violent notion of getting in there and fixing each other up that's so prevalent in Western culture. He provides a vision of restorative theology that does not rely on ultimate destruction as our end. But he affirms the possibility of how one might be present to a person's solitude, without getting in the way of God's deep work in a person's soul.[3]

Restorative theology challenges some of the basic interpretations of Christianity. The notion that even the most virulent sinner has a place in God's kingdom is often met with a wall of opposition. Restorative theology challenges one of the more important questions religion tries to answer: How are we saved? I think most of the great religions, counting on ultimate retributive justice, answer that question by saying that some are saved and some are damned. But this traditional answer to the question of human destiny is no longer meaningful for many people today, partly because people from the great religions are now meeting each other and discovering that the "other" may not be the devil after all.

"The idea that people from the other religions are going to hell just doesn't make sense anymore," say Mulholland and Gulley. Mulholland resigned from a pastoral post because of tensions created by the book. In 2001, Gulley was fired by Multnomah, a conservative Christian book publisher, when they learned he was working on the book. Christian bookstores cleared their shelves of his prior works and his sales plummeted by 80 percent. "According to them, Gulley had become heretical," Mulholland explained. "I'm sure they had economic fears, too. I think the Christian publishing world acts as a gatekeeper, and they decide what gets in and what doesn't get in. If you go to a Christian bookstore, it's already been screened pretty well."

Ty Inbody, professor of theology at United Theological Seminary of the Twin Cities in Minnesota, says, "Like the authors, I have discovered that this question arises for my students as an autobiographical conundrum before it becomes a theological quandary. It arises first as an intuitional problem, then as a theological problem. They simply find it impossible to accept the common interpretation of the church's teaching that only those who know God the way Christians know God will not be damned forever in a burning pit someplace with a ZIP code below the Earth's crust."[4]

On the opposing side are theologians such as Albert Mohler, president of the Southern Baptist Theological Seminary in Louisville, who wrote an essay saying the book was well written and well reasoned but "ultimately heretical and dangerous." Despite the criticism, Gulley and Mulholland are enjoying the buzz created by their book. Gulley, who dilutes much of the negative flack with a measured dose of humor, says any religion that causes people to love God and love their neighbors is an authentic and pure religion.[5]

To help you understand restorative theology more particularly, I offer a last set of questions for your consideration. These are particularly useful for group discussions. The purpose of the following questions is to open your creative imagination, to overcome provincial thinking, and to propose an ideal that can direct practical thought and action toward reconciliation. After all, reconciliation seeks to go beyond the way the world is and consider how it should and could be. An additional goal for you is to become aware of the resistance and barriers to a perfect world. Below is a survey of how you negotiate reconciliation *socially*. Answer the survey by either circling your closest answer of Y (yes), N (no), or P (possibly), or by providing a brief answer at the end of each question.

Restorative Theology as Utopian Vision

1. Does the religious body you belong to generate a vision of a future society congruent with a plan that includes practical steps to bring it about?   Y   N   P
2. As best you can recall, what is your religious body's official stance toward one of the following: racism, sexism, or the economy? If you cannot recall an official position, reflect on your personal relationship with your institutional church or religious group.   Y   N   P
3. What would a perfect society look like for your religious body—a utopia where there was absolutely no injustice or selfishness?   Y   N   P
4. What factors prevent your utopian vision?   Y   N   P

5. Would there still be racial, ethnic, and gender   Y N P
   differences in your utopia (e.g., would there be
   black and white people, gay and lesbian people,
   rich and poor people)?

6. Given your utopian ideal and the barriers to   Y N P
   such a utopia mentioned in question 4, what is
   the best practical world attainable (better than
   the current situation)?

7. What concrete strategies have your closest com-   Y N P
   munities (especially the church or religious
   group you belong to) proposed to move us
   from the present toward the ideal?

8. Are there concrete actions that your religious   Y N P
   organization could take to promote your
   utopian vision? If there are such actions, what
   other organizations are needed to make them
   occur?

This survey gives us language for discussing the problem of apocalyptic reconciliation when the question is asked: "Will only a few
be saved?" In particular, Luke states, "Jesus went through one town
and village after another, teaching as he made his way to Jerusalem.
Someone asked him, 'Lord, will only a few be saved?'" (Luke
13:23). Who will be saved was a constant obsession in the church
for centuries. Theologians and church officials interpreted scripture
passages such as this one from Luke to try to improve church members' chances for salvation, even to the selling of indulgences.

To become obsessive-compulsive about who is saved either at
the end of your individual time on earth or at the collective end of
life is to believe in a small god. You see, God is much bigger than
our imaginations can fathom. For example, eternity as a concept is
based on time being perpetual. But have you ever thought about
God's reality existing before anything else did? God created this
universe, including the stars and planets on which we conceptually
base time. In other words, God created eternity. This is good news
to us, because it helps us see beyond our obsession of who is saved

at the end of time: God's time is something we cannot fully understand, so God's salvation, too, can extend beyond what we think
we understand.

St. Paul gives us this vision to see beyond what we think we
understand:

> [O]bserve those who live according to the example you
> have in us. For many live as enemies of the cross of Christ;
> I have often told you of them, and now I tell you even with
> tears. Their end is destruction; their god is the belly; and
> their glory is in their shame; their minds are set on earthly
> things. But our citizenship is in heaven, and it is from
> there that we are expecting a Savior, the Lord Jesus Christ.
> *He will transform the body of our humiliation that it may be*
> *conformed to the body of his glory, by the power that also*
> *enables him to make all things subject to himself.* Therefore,
> my brothers and sisters, whom I love and long for, my joy
> and crown, stand firm in the Lord in this way, my beloved.
> (Philippians 3:17–4:1)

Paul teaches that God's power makes all things subject to God's
self. In other words, God will eventually be the subject of all of creation, even to those who have not yet made God subject.

The reason you read and I write this book is to spend time in
prayer reflecting on what God has accomplished—not necessarily
through us, but despite us. For Paul, our destiny is in Christ. This
was from the foundation of the world, that they should be made
holy by separation from sin, being set apart to God, and sanctified
by the Holy Spirit, in consequence of their election in Christ (para-
phrase, Ephesians 1:3–4). All who are chosen to happiness as the
end, are chosen to holiness as the means. In love they were predes-
tined, or foreordained, to be adopted as children of God by faith
in Christ Jesus, and to be openly admitted to the privileges of that
high relation to himself. The reconciled and adopted believer, the
pardoned sinner, is the one aware of God. God's love appointed

this method of knowledge of God. This method of grace gives no encouragement to evil, but shows sin in all its hatefulness. This is the gospel that turns the world upside down. Hostilities end. Enmities vanish. Strangers become friends. What could not be imagined—humanity controlled by love rather than by fear—is present! The peace that flows from grace is more than a spiritual condition of serenity; this peace is a living reality. Again, this is God's doing.

Whenever we read Ephesians, we are invited to enter a strange, new world: the world of God making all things new. Ephesians helps us see God's destiny for us. Perhaps we take ourselves too seriously in God's mission and forget that God is ultimately the one who gets us to our destination. Our job is to participate in what God is already doing, redeeming the world and moving us all toward salvation. The following story helps us take ourselves less seriously.

A couple was driving to a church to get married. On the way, they got into a car accident and died. When they arrive in heaven, they see St. Peter at the gate. They ask him if he could arrange it so they could marry in heaven. St. Peter tells them that he'll do his best to work on it for them.

Three months pass and the couple hears nothing. They bump into St. Peter and ask him about the marriage. He says, "I'm still working on it."

Two years pass by and no marriage. St. Peter again assures them that he's working on it.

Finally after twenty long years, St. Peter comes running with a priest and tells the couple it's time for their wedding. They marry and live happily for a while. But after a few months, they find St. Peter to tell him things are not working out, and that they want to get a divorce. "Can you arrange it for us?" they ask. St. Peter replies, "Are you kidding?! It took me twenty years to find a priest up here. How am I gonna find you a lawyer?"

God teaches a strange truth for us all; God asks us to imagine the unimaginable—that Jews and Gentiles both could end up in the same place. It is a world of borrowed forms and fresh beliefs. Every idea previously known and every truth previously affirmed is stretched to hold the new content of faith: Jesus Christ. The opening words of Ephesians are a fresh and uniquely Christian approach to the task of communicating faith in the first century: the language of worship. At times this language is grand and soaring. Profound phrases carry grand beliefs: "Blessed be the God and Father of our Lord Jesus Christ," "adopted as his children," "redemption through his blood." Poetic phrases reach, touch, and please the soul: the riches of grace, a plan for the fullness of time, living for the praise of his glory. These are worship words; they are profound and beautiful. Beneath these worshipful words, a melody rings. Paul has unfolded the work of Christ in reconciling the Jew and the Gentile.

The remarkable lesson from the third chapter of Ephesians is in Paul's demonstration of what I call a communal self who is capable of seeing such reconciliation. Paul learned to see himself as intimately linked to the miraculous work of being reconciled, so much so that he relativized his own suffering in the dire circumstances of his imprisonment and worried more about the survival of faith in a community (the Ephesian church) than about his personal safety or discomfort. Paul urges us toward movement of a communal self in three sections of chapter 3:

1. Paul describes the apostolic office as a communal identity (1–12).

It is as if Paul anticipates the interpersonal mysticism of Martin Buber's famous book *I and Thou* as he describes the interplay between his personal identity with the other. Paul says in the first verse: "I . . . for the sake of you. . . ." In the second verse he writes at the end of the sentence, "me for you." In verse 4, he describes the mystery of a community perceiving his personal identity. And in verses 5 and 6, Paul describes the greatest mystery of his life's work:

how those who were once unclean have become bonded to him. In verses 7–12, he describes his apostolic work within this new communal identity through paradox—that his good news (gospel) is in his servanthood to others. Annie Dillard in *Teaching a Stone to Talk* helps me describe this mysterious communal self. She writes:

> In the deeps are the violence and terror of which psychology has warned us. But if you ride these monsters deeper down, if you drop with them farther over the world's rim, you find what our sciences cannot locate or name, the substrate, the ocean or matrix or ether which buoys the rest, which gives goodness its power for good, and evil its power for evil, the unified field: our complex and inexplicable caring for each other, and for our life together here. This is given. It is not learned.[6]

I like Parker Palmer's interpretation of this Dillard passage. He says she teaches us that the spiritual journey moves downward, not upward toward abstraction. It moves downward toward the hardest concrete realities of our lives. Part of the gift of feminist spirituality is a reversal of what we traditionally understood spirituality to be, which was up and out—up, up, and away! Annie Dillard is saying that we must go in and down. And she's saying that on the way down and in, we will meet the violence and terror we have within ourselves that we project outwardly onto our institutions, onto our society.[7]

2. Paul sees his sole purpose as encouraging a despondent community (v. 13).

I think Paul and Annie Dillard have a lot in common. His going farther over the world's rim was to discover a communal self, one capable of seeing his own violence and terror so as not to perpetuate violence and terror in his community, thus encouraging those on the edge of losing hope.

3. Paul prays for the Ephesian community to grow in strength using an image of a tree deeply rooted in the soil (vv. 14–21).

Paul (and Dillard) also addresses movement toward the hardest concrete realities of our lives as he uses the vegetative imagery of a tree growing deeply within the soil. His goal is for the Ephesian community to grow from a fledgling and vulnerable community of individuals into a towering state, flourishing and strong—to reflect God through the Holy Spirit. The insight of Parker Palmer regarding the inner work of spirituality is helpful here: While inner work is a deeply personal matter, it is not necessarily a private one. There are ways to be together in community to help each other with that inner work. Quakers, in particular, come together in a way that is supportive but not invasive, asking a lot of questions but never rendering judgment or giving advice. Their togetherness respects the mystery of the human heart but still allows people to challenge and "stretch" one another in that work.

The following story gives us insight into accountability.

Two traveling angels stopped to spend the night in the home of a wealthy family. The family was rude and refused to let the angels stay in the mansion's guest room. Instead, the angels were given a small space in the cold basement. As they made their bed on the hard floor, the older angel saw a hole in the wall and repaired it When the younger angel asked why, the older angel replied, "Things aren't always what they seem."

The next night the pair came to rest at the house of a very poor but very hospitable farmer and his wife. After sharing what little food they had, the couple let the angels sleep in their bed where they could have a good night's rest. When the sun came up the next morning, the angels found the farmer and his wife in tears. Their only cow, whose milk had been their sole income, lay dead in the field. The younger angel was infuriated and asked the older angel how he could have let this happen. The first man had everything, yet you helped him, she accused. The second family had little but was willing to share everything, and you let the cow die.

"Things aren't always what they seem," the older angel replied. "When we stayed in the basement of the mansion, I noticed there was gold stored in that hole in the wall. Since the owner was so obsessed with greed and unwilling to share his good fortune, I sealed the wall so he wouldn't find it. Last night as we slept in the farmers bed, the angel of death came for his wife. I gave him the cow instead. Things aren't always what they seem."

Sometimes that is exactly what happens when things don't turn out the way they should. If you have faith, you just need to trust that every outcome is always to your advantage, because God will make all things subject to God's self. Of course you raise the question usually posed in our western worldview: What about human free will? Will God make our free will go away? No, in fact, by relentlessly inviting us into reconciliation, God increases our freedom—perfects it even. Serving God becomes our perfect freedom. You might not know it until some time later.

So, St. Paul tells us not to worry who gets into heaven:

But the righteousness that comes from faith says, "Do not say in your heart, 'Who will ascend into heaven?'" (that is, to bring Christ down) "or 'Who will descend into the abyss?'" (that is, to bring Christ up from the dead). But what does it say? "The word is near you, on your lips and in your heart" (that is, the word of faith that we proclaim). (Romans 10:6–8)

To think about heaven, one must imagine a perfect environment of community without conflict and yet one comprised of the fullness of difference created by God. In heaven there is a reordering around the life of God. The apocalyptic writer of Revelation writes, "I saw no temple in the city, for its temple is the Lord God the Almighty and the Lamb" (21:22). This is a beautiful image because, unlike exclusivist visions of heaven in which St. Peter stands at the gate to lock some out, the apocalyptic writer states, "Its gates will never be shut by day—and there will be no night there" (21:25). The writer even leaves open the hope for estranged cultures and ethnic people who are permanently wounded on earth to one day be healed: "[A]nd the leaves of the tree are for the healing of the nations [*ethnoi*]" (22:2). This vision culminates in a reordering of power and control. No longer is power in the hands of despots and tyrants. The writer of the apocalyptic revelation still had such a vision of power that he tried bowing down at the feet of an angel. But the writer was corrected: "I fell down to worship at the feet of the angel who showed them to me; but he said to me, 'You must not do that! I am a [mutual slave] with you'" (22:8-9).

The concept of heaven provides us with an understanding of mutual relationship as justice. The problem of heaven, however, is its idealism. But without idealism, we die. John Hope Franklin states, "You can't live if you're pessimistic. I don't think you can live. You can't function if you're pessimistic. You can't go on every day knowing or believing that things are not going to get better."[8] Christians are aware of the difficulty of keeping human attention fixed both on the divine realm and on social transformation of current realities. In fact, without attention to both heaven and social transformation, human beings will tend toward delusion or anarchy.

The topic of heaven is important in spiritual and mystical discourse because it reorients Western imagination to the understanding that people are made intentionally for mutuality. The deep insight of heaven is that our mutuality is what makes us live forever. By becoming reconcilers, we participate in God's reality—we practice "God's kingdom come" here on earth. As we accept and live in spiritual reality along with earthly reality, we avoid a capricious understanding of existence, a materialistic understanding of reality in which we resolve to ourselves that when we die—that's it! The phenomenon of reconciliation in the world, however, shows another reality. My hope in writing this book is that we all may learn to desire to pass beyond individualistic and materialistic existence into mutual participation with God, who knows how to make creation contain infinity. Instead of Western individualism, innate to the mystical language of heaven is the understanding of mutuality with God and creation. From spiritual practices of reconciliation, we learn, as a paradox and not as a contradiction: No one is born to die.

To think about heaven, we must imagine a perfect environment, a community without conflict where no one is hindered by being different. Such thoughts of heaven, ironically, provide the proper vision of how to live on earth. I argue that the demise of the concept of heaven and the beatific vision of God posited by some twentieth-century thinkers results in the demise of concepts of justice and peace.

In particular, I believe that human imaginings of heaven create a connatural reality between earth's "realized eschatology" and heaven's supernatural intervention. In other words, imagination continually shows us the goal of our createdness. God is both at the end of earth's journey and at its beginning, coaxing human nature to realize its distinction in God's self. Instead of violating our free will, God interacts with humanity in such a way as to facilitate clearer vision of who we are becoming. Therefore, imagination is a divine gift that enables human vision to see through the finality of earthly existence. This "seeing through" enables us to accept sacramental realities and move beyond the simple conclusion that life is inherently violent and finite. The practice of nonviolence demonstrates that attention to heaven is not delusional; instead, such heavenly imagination self-fulfills a tendency toward justice and peace and allows us to have a better vision of how to live here, now, on earth. Desmond Tutu relates such heavenly information to earthly justice in the following way:

> The tremendous thing about each one of us is that we have a value which is an infinite value. It resides in the very fact of being created and so we say to the perpetrators of racism and apartheid, your policies are immoral, are unchristian, are unbiblical. You are taking on God for you are saying, God has made a mistake, that God, when he

created some black, has made a ghastly mistake so that
they have to go around apologizing for their existence. We
don't have to apologize for our existence. God created us
in his own image.[9]

God's image makes us all infinite; herein, you and I may discover a definition of heaven. God's image is trinity. The nature of
the Trinity as God's being (*homoousios*) is not abstract divinity in a
rational essence binding three individuals (hypostases), for example, as the classification of reptile is common to a lizard and two
snakes. Instead, hypostasis is a term that leads us past the category
of anything individual such as snakes and lizards that are part of
the reptilian classification. There is no such fraction in God's
nature. Hypostases are infinitely united and infinitely different
because they are synchronically the divine nature as they uniquely
share each other's company. Such act and being I define as heaven.
     It is by persons opening up completely to one another that the
hypostases are able to share *homoousios* without restriction, without being divided. Outside of praise and adoration, outside of an
interpersonal relationship of faith, and outside of prayer, there can
be no habitation of God. My favorite Christian mystic, Simone
Weil, states, "The divine emptiness, fuller than fullness, has come
to inhabit us."[10] Following through the mystical procession of pur-
gation, illumination, and union, a person who experiences the
habitation of God must first experience a poverty of intellect in
which God lights upon the person who then discovers transformation from an impoverished self to the flourishing state of communal generosity.[11] Tutu illustrates such generosity:

> [W]e know by divine revelation that God is fullness of
> being, pulsating love from all eternity because God is a fel-
> lowship, a community, God is a society from all eternity in
> which God the Son, who is coequal, coeternal with the
> Father pours forth in return His entire love and being on the
> Father. The love that binds them together is so immense
> that this love flowing between Father and Son is God the

Holy Spirit. And so God created us wonderfully, not out of necessity. He did not need us; but gloriously, He wanted us. . . . We are privileged to be God's . . . eucharistic persons who hold everything in trust for God and who are forever saying thank you God for your generosity. We return to you what you have entrusted to us temporarily—our time, our money, our talents, our future lives. We are but responding to and seeking to reflect only your own lavish and magnificent generosity.[12]

Christian consciousness is formed by this narrative of God's interaction with creation whether people acknowledge God or not. Salvation is understood in our turning toward God whose presence cleanses our destructive desires. Therefore, reconciliation is not so much what we choose to do as it is what we become—clean in God. In reconciliation, the wound of creation is slowly transfigured toward a new heaven and earth.

This new heaven and earth become the environment of interpersonal vulnerability, in other words, a set of relationships in which people are able to recognize that their personhood is bound up in the other's humanity. Particular to his South African environment, Tutu imagines a heaven to appeal to his society to move beyond racial distinctions as determinative of human identity. As Tutu states further: "We have in this land a pyramid of power and privilege based on color—the lighter you are of pigmentation, the higher you stand on the pyramid of privilege and power. In this pyramid blacks are the broad base of the exploited and oppressed. Next is the so called colored and then next Indians and right at the top Makulubaas, white. It is a pigmentocracy."[13] Through heavenly imagination, in which human identity is elevated as persons find communion with others and God, restorative theology makes sense of how South Africans should then proceed to operate on the basis of more than racial identity. In other words, people need not kill each other because they are black or white, but should instead rejoice in how God has created persons differently so that new meanings and identities are always possible.

CHAPTER 8
A New Heaven and Earth

[Jesus said to the criminal on the cross], "Truly I tell you, today you will be with me in Paradise."

—Luke 23:43

Jesus was resurrected right before their eyes. The resurrected Jesus even ate fish at a barbeque with the disciples (John 21:9–14). So, what does this tell us about a new heaven and earth? I think it tells us this: God's intentional love is to make us mutual persons never abstracted from where we are and who we are. By inhabiting God's ways of reconciling the world, we all concede the need to be transformed into a new identity, a new perspective that fully encompasses reconciliation. As Tutu states, "God does not love us because we are lovable, but we are lovable precisely because God loves us. God's love is what gives us our worth. . . . So we are liberated from the desire to achieve, to impress. We are the children of the divine love and nothing can change that fundamental fact about us."[1] And yet, as Tutu's theology unfolds, providing access to a new identity for South Africans, it also appeals to ancient African concepts of the harmony between individual and community that John Mbiti describes: "I am because we are, and since we are, therefore I am."[2] God intends to transfigure and transform the world so that it will not disappear into nothingness but will enter the dimensions of the new heaven and earth when all manner of things will be made well. Caught up in this end, the church is called to participate with God in this exhilarating enterprise of transfiguration so that what is in bondage to corruption will be liberated as it groans to be made complete. The whole of creation groans in expectancy of a new creation. Tutu concludes:

> Clearly the entire situation cried out for atonement, for re-unification. . . . And so we could say that the story of the Bible which is the story of our deliverance is the story of the quest for that primeval unity. It is a deep yearning for integration, for harmony, for fellowship, for unity, for communion. Consequently, the descriptions of the end time, the time of the consummation, the eschatological time when the kingdoms of this world would become the Kingdom of our God and His Christ, we hear echoes of the descriptions of the beginning times recorded in the Pentateuch, the paradisal times when Adam lived in harmony with all creation (Genesis 2:8–20, cf. Isaiah 11:6–9).[3]

Proper attention to heaven produces the desire for justice; in other words, true attention to God disallows the treatment of others as means for ends. Tutu states:

> [A]t the heart of things is an ultimate reality that is good and loving, concerned to see that justice and goodness and love will prevail. This ultimate reality I believe to be personal, a being with whom I can enter into intimate personal relationship. Despite all appearances to the contrary this ultimate reality, God is in charge, but in charge in a way that does not cancel out our autonomy as persons. God gives us space to be persons who are moral agents, with the capacity to respond freely, to love or not to love, to obey or not to obey, free to be good or to be vicious.

God has such a profound reverence for our autonomy and
freedom that He had much rather see us go freely to hell
than compel us to go to heaven. As they say, the doctrine
of hell is God's greatest complement to us as humans.[4]

In the end, our inhabitation of God collapses hierarchy that engen-
ders the idea of retributive justice. Thus, the opposite of hierarchy
is not, as the revolutionists believe, equality, but anarchy; for when
hierarchy is disrupted, there is a violent oscillation between one
form of inequality and another, issuing in a confusion that may be
mistaken for adjustment or "progress." Uprooting people and
dumping them as rubbish puts an end to every vestige of natural
equality; it is the condition of being rootless which was the impe-
tus of the oppressor in implementing apartheid. Rootlessness is
the most severe form of affliction.[5] Thanks be to God that there is
someone we can hold on to.

Christ reveals the salvation of the world, but such a revelation
does not require control or domination on our part, neither does
it claim a banal observation of a "new heaven and new earth"
already complete on earth. Instead, God created us to be responsible
for each other and ourselves; in fact, to know one's identity through
others becomes a way to a new heaven and earth. This is so because
God desired that our movement toward God's life be a movement of
participation in the divine life, a life that implies freedom. As
Gregory of Nyssa (c. 335–386) states: "As the grace of God cannot
descend upon souls which flee from their salvation, so the power of
human virtue is not of itself sufficient to raise to perfection souls
which have no share in grace . . . the righteousness of works and the
grace of the Spirit, coming together to the same place . . . fill the soul
in which they are united with the life of the blessed."[6]

The story of the fall reminds us that our control of the knowledge of good and evil is only partial. If we take a dualistic view of
evil, then we not only compound our futile grasping at knowledge
that is beyond our creatureliness, but we create a hierarchy in which
humans identify themselves according to superior races, genders,
and socioeconomic classes. It is even more insidious when such a

hierarchy becomes implicitly defined as God's created order. We cannot fully know the mystery of God. We can only be wounded by it as we choose it, do it, and suffer from it, and even then, we must not presume that we know what is and what is not evil from God's perspective.

Most important in our vision of heaven is that God does not remain inaccessible, like some Aristotelian unmoved mover. God emptied himself and became involved with suffering people, even when they were cast into the fiery furnace. Then the oppressors saw a fourth and mysterious figure walking about with the three that were originally thrown there (Daniel 3:24–27). The Old Testament, having struggled with the problem of righteous suffering, reaches a zenith in the so-called Songs of the Suffering Servant of Yahweh, especially in Isaiah (52:13–53:12). The text describes vicarious suffering, suffering not for one's sake but on behalf of others, even on behalf of others for their salvation. Herein Tutu takes solace that there is a redeeming value for how black people have suffered, that perhaps here, with the Suffering Servant, there is a clue about the inevitability of suffering in the economy of salvation. Tutu defends God's goodness despite the suffering of black Africans, saying that their severe suffering is not in vain and that suffering has salvific significance.

There is identity and solidarity with the Suffering Servant in the New Testament as well, an identification that occurred when Jesus agreed to be baptized. The event caused some a theological problem, as can be seen in the conversation that Matthew records as having taken place between John the Baptist and Jesus (3:6, cf. 3:13–16). For if John's baptism was an acknowledgment of sin, how could the sinless one need to be baptized? We are again in the realm of mystery, the mystery of what it cost God to redeem us. Which one of us can know what it meant for the all holy, perfect man to be so close to sin that he had to utter that awful cry of dereliction, "My God, my God, why have you forsaken me?" (Mark 15:33–36).

Since Jesus did not enter glory without suffering, and his glory accomplished the salvation of the world, the followers of this Jesus have no other way to Easter and the ascension except through the gateway of passion and crucifixion, through Good Friday (Matthew 10:24–25). Jesus makes it abundantly clear that discipleship without suffering is impossible (Matthew 10:17–39). Unless the disciple takes up the cross and follows, then there is no discipleship.

With our attention to God's presence in heaven, we are enabled to discover how to become enough of a person to commune with God. This view, becoming enough of a person, safeguards our anthropomorphic tendencies of making an abstracted polis into heaven. In other words, human imagination is the corrective humility that, in the world, the search of the human soul for heaven is really the effort of staying awake as a person in the presence of God rather than existing merely as an animal. Lack of belief in the immortality of human beings cannot but affect the way we think and talk about the Christian life. Confession of sin is unintelligible apart from the acknowledgment of who you are. And who you are is not complete without the beatific vision of cohabitation with God. Confession that we harm persons, not objects, makes intelligible our mysterious struggle toward immortality.

The struggle is that we forget who we are, and we take each other for granted. In so doing, we take the image of God in vain. We take God's name in vain when we forget the image of God among us. Perhaps there is no literary writer better at articulating how we take God's name in vain than Flannery O'Connor in her short story "Revelation."[7]

Mrs. Ruby Turpin, a "very large," respectable, and church-going woman with a self-deprecating sense of humor, has brought her husband Claud to the doctor's office to be treated for a leg ailment. The doctor's small waiting room is almost full when they arrive. As gospel music plays softly in the background, Ruby takes center stage among the people there. Indeed, both her physical size and her personal presence virtually overtake the room. Full of self-certainty about the other people in the room, she even classifies them by the shoes they wear. Ruby has a habit of classifying others; when she has trouble falling asleep at night, she calms herself by imagining all the classes of people.

On the bottom of the heap were most colored people, not the kind she would have been if she had been one, but most of them; then next to them—not above, just away from—were the white trash; then above them were the homeowners, and above them the home-and-land owners, to which she and Claud belonged. Above her and Claud were people with a lot of money and much bigger houses and much more land.

Ruby is not simply content to classify people in the context of her own smug self-contentment. She begins to hurl around well-mannered comments—actually, carefully disguised but sharply barbed insults, even observing that her pigs are cleaner than some children she has seen. Ruby's arrogance is based on a self-righteous judgment in which faults consistently lie with others, not herself. O'Connor writes that Ruby is grateful that Jesus "had not made her a nigger or white-trash or ugly! He had made her herself and given her a little of everything. Jesus, thank you! She said."

There is one college girl in the room, however, who Ruby is not able to dismiss as easily as she does the rest of them. Mary Grace is home from Wellesley and sits in the doctor's waiting room reading a book entitled *Human Development*. Ruby notices how ugly the girl is, that she wears Girl Scout shoes, and that she seems to be filled with contempt for just about everybody—including, unfortunately, Ruby. As Ruby is in the midst of replicating her chorus of thanksgiving to Jesus for "making everything the way it is," Mary Grace strikes Ruby just over the left eye with the book *Human Development*.

Before Ruby can utter a sound, Mary Grace wrestles Ruby to the floor. Ruby looks into Mary Grace's fiercely maniacal eyes with "no doubt in her mind that the girl did know her, knew her in some intense and personal way, beyond time and place and condition." It was this knowledge that made Mary Grace's judgment, and her final words to Ruby, even more severe: "Go back to hell where you came from, you old wart hog."

As Ruby struggles with the judgment, she returns to her old system of justifying herself by judging others. But even that fails her now, and her protests take on almost a comic quality as she discovers that she has taken God for granted. As she looks up, Ruby discovers that the scathing judgment she has received has been nothing less than God's redeeming grace. She sees a purple streak in the sky leading into the descending dusk.

> A visionary light settled in her eyes. She saw the streak as a vast swinging bridge extending upward from the earth through a field of living fire. Upon it a vast horde of souls were rumbling toward heaven. There were whole companies of white-trash, clean for the first time in their life, and bands of black niggers in white robes, and battalions of freaks and lunatics shouting and clapping and leaping like frogs. And bringing up the end of the procession was a tribe of people whom she recognized at once as those who, like herself and Claud, had always had a little of everything and the God-given wit to use it right. She leaned forward to observe them closer. They were marching behind the others with great dignity, accountable as they had always been for good order and common sense and respectable behavior. They alone were on key. Yet she could see by their shocked and altered faces that even their virtues were being burned away. (508)

Ruby's vision of the restoration of persons now includes herself. Further, she is no longer judge of others or even the "first" among people; people like her move through the field of living fire, and even then their virtues are being burned away. She no longer takes God's name in vain because she has a beatific vision. The context of Ruby's vision of the kingdom is clear; none of us can escape divine judgment. Yet, as Ralph Wood has rightly pointed out, here "divine wrath is couched wholly in terms of divine mercy. It is a mercy that is like a refiner's fire—cleansing rather than consuming."[8] Our struggle toward immortality must go through this cleansing fire.

It is this purging, sanctifying character of the "living fire" of God's Holy Spirit that makes Ruby's vision a sign of God's grace rather than simply a consuming destruction. Despite the clarity of Ruby's eschatological vision, the story does not simply end there. She returns to her house along a "darkening path." As her sight fades, she notices that invisible cricket choruses have struck up; but what she hears are "the voices of the souls clinging upward into the starry field and shouting hallelujah" (509). Here the story ends, reminding us that though our vision of God's kingdom is important and indeed central, we must nevertheless learn to live in this time between the times as "through a glass, darkly" (1 Corinthians 13:12 KJV).

O'Connor's story presents a stark contrast to our normal practices of reconciliation. Ruby Turpin might have been very willing to forgive others in particular instances, and perhaps even to forget. After all, she considered herself a very "religious" person. But self-interested reconciliation would simply have reinforced Ruby's own self-certainty and self-righteousness. Ruby is absolutely convinced of the truthfulness of her observations, all the while standing in self-righteous judgment of others. Self-interested spirituality offers Ruby no resources for coming to terms with her own self-deception.

Furthermore, when Ruby does learn to see things differently, it is not by putting on the "magic eyes" of seeing ourselves simply as "weak, needy, and fallible." Rather, she learns to see differently through an encounter with the purifying fire of God's judgment of grace, a fire that forces Ruby to acknowledge her own sin and need of grace. It is not a question of forgiving herself, or even of forgiving God. Ruby could not forgive herself because one of the identifying features of her character is self-deception. That is, she fails to see herself as she really is until she has to come to terms with the judgment of God as found in Mary Grace. And though Ruby may have found it psychologically comforting to forgive God for this hurt she has received, it would have been thoroughly inadequate. For what Ruby really needs is not the psychological comfort of forgiving God for hurts she feels she does not deserve (and wondering if God would mind!), but rather an encounter with God's judgment of grace, which enables her to see herself and her world more truthfully.

Ruby's story alludes to the parable of Jesus that is often identi-
fied as the parable of the Prodigal Son (Luke 15:11–32). A better
title would be the parable of the Forgiving Father. The focus is not
so much on either of the ungrateful sons as on the character of the
father, who joyously forgives and receives both of his children back
into his fellowship.

Like Ruby, the younger son only comes to himself by comparing his own existence to that of contented pigs. He has deceived
himself by thinking that life and the self are things to be possessed.
In the pigsty, he realizes that his life has been dissipated in his
attempt to control it. But in that recognition he also discovers
that the father gives and forgives him. He does not forgive himself; indeed, he is prepared to punish himself by becoming one
of his father's hired workers. Nor does he forgive his father; he
realizes that the father has not done anything for which he
would be culpable. But he does discover his father's prior forgiveness, which celebrates his return and creates a changed context for his future.

But the older son is no better off by the end of the parable. He
also sees life in terms of possession, and he is outraged at the
breach of fairness and justice. While he has not squandered his
inheritance, he assumes that he possesses a righteousness based on
his fidelity. But, like Ruby Turpin, his is a false way of being
upright, a stance that is unable to bend the body in gestures of
love, to acknowledge the gift that others, including the Other who
is God, offer to him. The father does not see human life as the sons
see it. They see it as a possession, but he sees it as a gift that must
be continually given—even at the cost of forgiveness.[9]

The revelation of the judgment of grace that comes to Ruby, like
the revelations that the two sons receive in Jesus' parable, suggests
that forgiveness is a free gift and that its purpose is the restoration
of communion with God and with others in Christian community
and the re-creation of human life with holiness as its destiny. But
this forgiveness is inseparable both from the judgment that challenges human self-deception and from the repentance that becomes

possible as we learn to see ourselves more clearly, as St. Thérèse of Lisieux discusses in her autobiography, *The Story of a Soul*:

> I had striven above all to love God, and in loving Him I discovered the secret of those other words "Not everyone who says Lord, Lord shall enter into the kingdom of heaven, but the one who does the will of my Father." Jesus made me understand what the will was by the words he used at the Last Supper when He gave His "new commandment" and told His apostles "to love one another as He had loved them." . . . When God under the old law told His people to love their neighbors as themselves. He had not yet come down to earth. As God knows how much we love ourselves, he could not ask us to do more. But when Jesus gave His apostles a "new commandment, His own commandment," He did not ask only that we should love our neighbors as ourselves, but that we should love them as He loves them and as He will love them to the end of time. O Jesus, I know you command nothing that is impossible . . . O Jesus ever since its gentle flame has consumed my heart, I have run with delight along the way of your "new commandment."[10]

NOTES

Chapter 1: Reconciling a Violent World

1. Anglican Communion Office, "Out of the Dust," ACNS 2749, November 2001, http://www.anglicancommunion.org/archive/html.

Chapter 2: A Typology of Reconciliation

1. For a fuller account of Tutu's restorative spirituality, see his book *No Future without Forgiveness* (New York: Doubleday, 2000).

2. I am indebted to Wilfrid Harrington for these insights into the Prodigal Son narrative. *Parables Told by Jesus: A Contemporary Approach* (New York: Alba House, 1974).

Chapter 3: Inhabiting Reconciliation

1. Richard Mouw, "Why the Evangelical Church Needs the Liberal Church," *Sojourners*, February 2004.

2. I am indebted here to the Jewish theologian David Blumenthal's definition of reconciliation. Blumenthal offers us additional insight into interreligious reconciliation by suggesting

we must first understand how the other religion understands the process of reconciliation. See David Blumenthal, "Repentance and Forgiveness," *Cross Currents* 48, no. 1 (Spring 1998).

3. Mouw, "Why the Evangelical Church Needs the Liberal Church," 15–16.

4. Clarissa Pinkola Estés, *Women Who Run with the Wolves: Myths and Stories of the Wild Woman Archetype* (New York: Ballantine, 1992).

5. George Herbert, "Love III," *The Temple: Sacred Poems and Private Ejaculations*, ed. N. Ferrar (Cambridge: T. Buck & R. Daniel, 1633). For recreation of Herbert poem, see eir.library.utoronto.ca/rpo/display/poem979.html.

6. Susan Vanzanten Gallagher, *Truth and Reconciliation: The Confessional Mode in South African Literature* (Portsmouth, NH: Heinemann, 2002), 206ff.

7. See Robert Enright and Joanna North, eds. (with foreword from Archbishop Desmond Tutu), *Exploring Forgiveness* (Madison: University of Wisconsin Press, 1998).

Chapter 4: Crossing the Threshold of Reconciliation

1. David Wood, interview with Albert Borgmann, "Primetime: Albert Borgmann on Taming Technology," *Christian Century*, August 23, 2003, 22.

2. Robert Johnson, *Owning Your Own Shadow: Understanding the Dark Side of the Psyche* (San Francisco: Harper SanFrancisco, 1993).

3. Lawrence Wright, *Noriega: God's Favorite*, directed by Roger Spottiswoode (Showtime & Regency Enterprises Film, 2000).

Chapter 5: Remembering God

1. C. S. Lewis, *The Weight of Glory* (New York: Macmillan, 1949), 14–15.

2. Tinyiko Sam Maluleke, "Can Lions and Rabbits Reconcile? The South African TRC as an Instrument for Peace-Building," *Ecumenical Review* 53, no. 2 (April 2001): 191.

3. This is from my notes from when I lived with Archbishop Tutu from 1993–1994, 21.

4. Maluleke, "Can Lions and Rabbits Reconcile," 197.

5. Maggie Ross, *Pillars of Flame: Power, Priesthood, and Spiritual Maturity* (San Francisco: Harper & Row, 1988), xxv.

6. Dom Helder Camera, address delivered April 12, 1964, quoted in Jose de Bracker, *Dom Helder Camera: The Violence of a Peacemaker* (Maryknoll, NY: Orbis, 1970), 102.

7. The Greek *katallaghv*, transliterated as *katallage*. Other important New Testament passages that deal with reconciliation are Romans 5:11 and Colossians 1:20–22. There seem to be two connotations for *katallage*. The first indicates an economic exchange, as between moneychangers who reconcile accounts. The second use refers to the restoration of relationships between God and humanity. It is the second connotation that I assume here.

8. Stanley Hauerwas, prayer for a vigil against the death penalty, April 16, 2002, Durham, North Carolina 27708. Used by permission.

9. E. J. Dionne Jr., "Faith, Politics, and the Common Good," *Religion and Values in Public Life* 6, no. 2/3 (Winter/Spring 1998): 2.

Chapter 6: Practicing God's Ways

1. Jay Price, "Epithet Shows Cultural Divide: Troops Turn Title of Respect into 'Trivializing' Slur for Iraqis, Others," *Raleigh (NC) News & Observer*, September 30, 2003, section A, 1.

2. My adaptation of John Donne, "Meditation 17" (1623–1624), from *Devotions upon Emergent Occasions* (New York: Vintage, 1997). See www.anglicanlibrary.org/donne/devotions/devotions17.htm.

3. Mouw, "Why the Evangelical Church Needs the Liberal Church," 16.

4. John Shelby Spong, question and answer session, February 12, 2004, *A New Christianity for a New World*, johnshelbyspong.com.

5. Willis Jenkins, "Mission as Reconciling Practice" (paper presented at Episcopal House of Bishops meeting, Camp Allen, TX, March 23, 2004).

6. Kerry Walters, *Jacob's Hip: Finding God in an Anxious Age* (Maryknoll, NY: Orbis, 2003), 1.

7. Ibid., 2.

8. Ibid., 5–7.

9. Martin Luther King Jr., *The Words of Martin Luther King, Jr.* (New York: Newmarket Press, 1981), 21.

Chapter 7: Reconciliation as God's Apocalypse

1. Alice Walker quoted in Maria Harris, "Jubilee Forgiveness," *Millennium Monthly*, April 2000, 1.

2. Philip Gulley and James Mulholland, *If Grace Is True: Why God Will Save Every Person* (New York: HarperSanFrancisco, 2003).

3. Rainer Maria Rilke (1875–1926), *Letters to a Young Poet* (New York: Random House, 1984).

4. Khalid Moss, "Authors Argue That Heaven Is Open to All Mankind," Cox News Service, *News & Observer*, December 26, 2003, Lifestyle, 1.

5. Ibid.

6. Annie Dillard, *Teaching a Stone to Talk: Expeditions and Encounters* (New York: Harper & Row, 1982), 94–95.

7. Parker Palmer, *Leading from Within: Reflections on Spirituality and Leadership* (Washington, DC: Servant Leadership, 1992), 9.

8. John Hope Franklin is a distinguished writer and professor emeritus of African American History at Duke University. We discussed this problem of pessimism over lunch at the Duke University Club, Durham, North Carolina, in the summer of 2001.

9. Desmond Tutu, "Birmingham Cathedral Address," from Tutu's personal files during my residence with him, 1993–1994, 3. See my book, *Reconciliation: The Ubuntu Theology of Desmond Tutu* (Cleveland: Pilgrim, 1997).

10. Simone Weil, *Gravity and Grace* (New York: Putnam, 1952), 41. See also E. W. F. Tomlin, *Simone Weil* (New Haven: Yale University Press, 1954), especially 53ff.

11. Catherine La Cugna, *God for Us: The Trinity and the Christian Life* (New York: HarperSanFrancisco, 1992), 1.

12. Desmond Tutu, handwritten sermon, St. George's Cathedral, August 21, 1986. Tutu goes on to give an illustration about the necessity of giving for life, just as one who only receives finds death, just like the Dead Sea, in which nothing can survive as it only receives its current. First Corinthians 4:7 seems to be the text of sermon: "For who sees anything different in you? What do you have that you did not receive? And if you received it, why do you boast as if it were not a gift?"

13. Tutu, handwritten address no. 5, no date.

Chapter 8: A New Heaven and Earth

1. Desmond Tutu, handwritten sermon, delivered on Christmas 1984, St. Philip's, Washington, DC.

2. John Mbiti, *African Religions and Philosophies* (New York: Doubleday, 1970), 141.

3. Desmond Tutu, "The Marks of the Church," from Tutu's personal files during my residence with him. See also my book, *Reconciliation: The Ubuntu Theology of Desmond Tutu* (Cleveland: Pilgrim, 1997).

4. Tutu, "Credo," 234. See also my book, *Reconciliation*.

5. See Weil, *Gravity and Grace*, especially 49ff.

6. Gregory of Nyssa, quoted in Vladimir Lossky, *The Mystical Theology of the Eastern Church* (London: Clarke, 1957), 197.

7. "Revelation," *The Complete Stories of Flannery O'Connor* (New York: Farrar, Straus, & Giroux, 1977), 488–509. I am indebted here to Greg Jones's discussion of O'Connor in his book, *Embodying Forgiveness* (Grand Rapids: Eerdmans, 1995).

8. Ralph Wood, *The Comedy of Redemption* (Notre Dame, IN: University of Notre Dame, 1988), 131.

9. For further discussion of this point, see Jean-Luc Marion, *God without Being*, trans. Thomas A. Carlson (Chicago: University of Chicago, 1991), 99.

10. Thérèse de Lisieux (1873–1897), *Story of a Soul: The Autobiography of St. Thérèse of Lisieux* (Washington, DC: ICS Publications, 1996), 37.

BIBLIOGRAPHY

Armstrong, Karen. *The Battle for God.* New York: Ballantine Books, 2000. Account of fundamentalist movements in the three Abrahamic traditions.

Augustine of Hippo. *The City of God.* In *Nicene and Post-Nicene Fathers of the Christian Church,* series 1, vol. 2. An important work to envision God's reconciled world.

Battle, Michael. *Reconciliation: The Ubuntu Theology of Desmond Tutu.* Cleveland, OH: Pilgrim Press, 1997. Focus on understanding human identity in relationship to community.

Douglas, Ian, and Kwok Pui-Lan, eds. *Beyond Colonial Anglicanism: The Anglican Communion in the Twenty-First Century.* New York: Church Publishing, 2001. Fifteen authors from throughout the Anglican Communion offer perspectives on relationships and opportunities within the global context.

Griswold, Frank T. *Going Home: An Invitation to Jubilee.* Cambridge: Cowley, 2001. The homilies and other papers delivered by the Presiding Bishop on the Jubilee theme of the Episcopal Church General Convention.

Helmick, Raymond G., and Rodney L. Peterson. *Forgiveness and Reconciliation: Religion, Public Policy, and Conflict Transformation.*

117

Philadelphia: Templeton Foundation Press, 2001. Definitive work on theology of reconciliation with practical experience in public policy and conflict transformation.

Tutu, Desmond. *No Future without Forgiveness*. New York: Doubleday, 1999. A bold spirituality that links truth-telling and reconciliation. Explores a vision for the future made possible by forgiveness.

Volf, Miroslov. *Exclusion and Embrace: A Theological Exploration of Identity, Otherness, and Reconciliation*. Nashville: Abingdon, 1996. An extremely helpful theological account of thinking through reconciliation.

Wallis, Jim. *The Soul of Politics*. Maryknoll, NY: Orbis, 1994. The founding editor of *Sojourners* offers an approach to mobilizing the religious community around issues of economic justice, racism, and peacemaking.

Wheatley, Margaret J. *Turning to One Another: Simple Conversations to Restore Hope to the Future*. San Francisco: Berrett-Koehler Publishers, 2002. The author of two award-winning books, *Leadership and the New Science* and *A Simpler Way*, turns her experience with organizations and community development to the promise of simple, honest, and human conversation as a discipline to provide hope for the future.

Williams, Rowan. *Writing in the Dust: After September 11*. Grand Rapids: Eerdmans, 2002. A challenging and uncomfortable reflection on the author's own experience on September 11, raising serious spiritual and ethical concerns.

Organizations Practicing Reconciliation

Episcopalians for Global Reconciliation
(See especially their 0.7% commitment to alleviate global poverty)
Zero Garden St.
Cambridge, MA 02138
Tel: (617) 876-0200
Web: episcopalglobalreconciliation.org

Fellowship of Reconciliation (FOR): Interfaith Peace-Builders
(See especially their pilgrimages to difficult areas of the world and historic memberships by Martin Luther King Jr. and Reinhold Niebuhr)
4545 42nd St. NW Suite 209
Washington, DC 20016
Tel: (202) 244-0821
Fax: (202) 244-6396
Web: forusa.org